TOFU TASTY

IMAGINATIVE TOFU RECIPES FOR EVERY DAY

BONNIE CHUNG

PHOTOGRAPHY BY YUKI SUGIURA

PAVILION

First published in the United Kingdom in 2021 by
Pavilion
43 Great Ormond Street
London WC1N 3HZ

ISBN 978-1-911663-29-4

A CIP catalogue record for this book is available from
the British Library.

10 9 8 7 6 5 4 3 2 1

Reproduction by Rival Colour Ltd, UK
Printed and bound by 1010 Printing International Ltd, China

www.pavilionbooks.com

Publisher: Helen Lewis
Editor: Sophie Allen
Design Manager: Laura Russell
Photographer: Yuki Sugiura
Production Manager: Phil Brown

CONTENTS

INTRODUCTION

Reliable, versatile and essential, my kitchen is never without tofu. It's my go-to pantry saviour for so many last-minute dinners and I eat it almost every day in one of its many forms.

Tofu has experienced a true renaissance in this new era of plant-based eating, as we search for more sustainable sources of protein. If you have picked up this cookbook, you might be familiar with tofu already; maybe you've tried a few dishes at home or in a restaurant and are looking for more recipe ideas. This is a really exciting time for tofu, and I hope to share inspiration for cooking it with confidence, as well as some recipes for making different types of tofu from scratch.

In this book, I hope to expand your tofu horizons, sharing with you the many different types and the multitude of ways in which you can cook it. You'll find all my favourite dishes, which I hope will make their way, quickly and firmly, into your cooking repertoire.

Tofu comes in so many different forms; the basic tofu blocks with which we are all familiar are just the tip of the iceberg. We will be exploring fermented tofu – squidgy and feta-like with a deep tangy flavour – and light, delicate, dried tofu, like twists of paper that rehydrate to a satisfying chew, among very many others. You will never be stuck in a tofu rut again.

In Asia, its spiritual home, tofu is not a meat alternative. Rather, it stands proudly in its own right. When I was growing up, tofu was an essential dish on the dinner table, along with fish, meat and vegetables, and sometimes the tofu would be cooked together with meat or seafood too; it didn't *replace* anything. In fact, if it was missing, someone would ask if it had been left in the kitchen. This book includes both classic tofu dishes from across Asia – picking the best from Japan, China and Korea – and other dishes of my own invention. I love mixing up traditional and modern techniques and flavours.

This book is organized into seven chapters to distinguish between the different types and textures of tofu; we have crispy dishes, soft steamed dishes, stir-fries, braised dishes and even desserts. All the recipes are vegetarian to start with, then I suggest added twists that may include meat, fish and other swaps, as you prefer. This gives you a strong foundation to build from and, if you are cutting out or cutting down on meat, you can simply make the base recipe. My recipes aim to draw out our main ingredient's original flavours and textures through the use of *contrast*. Juxtaposing sharp heat, acidity and crunch brings out tofu's natural character, highlighting its calm, sweet beanyness.

I have lost count of the number of people who have been converted to tofu after tasting some of these dishes, so, wherever you are on your tofu discovery journey, I hope you will join me in enjoying and sharing these dishes too.

If you have any preconceptions about what tofu is like, forget them… Start again with *Tofu Tasty*.

TOFU EXPLAINED

Fresh tofu is made from curds of soya milk that have usually been pressed firmly into compact blocks. To make it, dried soya beans are soaked in water, then ground with fresh water to create soya milk. The solid residue of the beans is then strained out before the milk is heated and a coagulant added to set it into curds. The set curds can be eaten as they are, or pressed to get rid of excess water and made into firm blocks.

At this stage, different types of tofu can be created, depending on the ratio of water to beans, the amount of coagulant used and how firmly the tofu is pressed. Then, once the tofu has been set, further types can be created: dried tofu, fermented tofu and deep-fried tofu – to name just a few.

THE MANY TYPES OF TOFU

The world of tofu is incredibly diverse. Flavours range from delicate to pungent, while textures start from melt-in-the-mouth and graduate through every stage up to firm and chewy. No matter what your preferred tastes, I am certain that there must be at least one type for everyone! The descriptions on the following pages will give you an initial sense of the different forms of tofu and how they are best enjoyed.

SOAK DRIED SOYA BEANS

GRIND INTO A PURÉE AND MIX WITH WATER

SOYA MILK

BOIL AND ADD A COAGULANT
SUCH AS NIGARI

SILKEN TOFU

THE COAGULANT IS ADDED
AFTER THE SOYA MILK IS
COMPLETELY CHILLED, NEVER
WHEN HOT. THE WHEY AND
CURDS AND THIS THICKER MILK
SETS TO FORM SILKEN TOFU.

CURDLED TOFU

THE CURDS SEPARATE
FROM THE WHEY

PRESS AND SET
THE TOFU

DRIED TOFU

THE TOP LAYER OF HOT
SOYA MILK IS SKIMMED OFF
AND DRIED IN SHEETS

FERMENTED TOFU

FRESH TOFU IS SEASONED
AND SUSPENDED IN A BRINE
TO FERMENT

FRESH TOFU

THE FIRMNESS LEVEL DEPENDS ON THE
AMOUNT OF NIGARI ADDED AND THE
PRESSURE AND LENGTH OF PRESSING. THIS
MAKES FIRM AND MEDIUM TOFU.

**ATSUAGE, ABURAAGE
OR TOFU PUFFS**

FRESH TOFU IS SEASONED
AND DEEP-FRIED

TOFU TYPE	KEY CHARACTERISTICS	PREPARATION	IDEAL DISHES
Fresh firm tofu	Dense blocks sold in water baths. Firm to the touch and easy to handle, with a little bounce to the texture. Very versatile.	For most stir-fries this tofu does not need pressing and it is robust enough to be moved in the pan without breaking. For crispy pan-fried dishes, coat with a little cornflour (corn starch), rice flour or plain flour and fry until golden before adding other flavours. For minced dishes, really squeeze out all the water before cooking and wrap in kitchen paper (paper towels) to absorb excess liquid.	Pan-fried crispy dishes Stir-fries Minced, for burger patties and dumpling fillings Baked recipes
Fresh soft or medium tofu	Similar to firm tofu but with a bouncier, softer and more porous texture. Absorbs a lot of flavour.	If you wish to use this type of tofu for a pan-fry or stir-fry, then pressing it is essential, or the tofu will break easily. There is no need to press the tofu if you're planning to use it for curries, scrambles and soups; just draining it is sufficient, as you want to retain its original texture.	Scrambled tofu Curries Soups
Ambient or fresh silken tofu	Wobbly and delicate with plain or egg flavours. This usually comes in a cardboard carton or, if fresh, packaged in a water bath.	Drain; no need to press. This type of tofu is fragile to cut, so care is needed in the handling.	Hotpots and stews Loading with sauces and pickles Soups Desserts
Fresh, pressed tofu	Very firm, compact tofu that is rubbery in texture, similar to halloumi cheese. Difficult to penetrate with new flavours, so often comes pre-infused with other flavours.	No need to press; simply slice it to the desired size. Ready for straight-to-wok stir-fries. As the texture is hard to penetrate with new tastes, it's best cooked with bold flavours to contrast with the tofu pieces.	Popular in the West for stir-fries or pan-fries due to its pre-pressed convenience and super-firm texture. Also great for chunky burgers and baked dishes. In Chinese cuisine, smoked pressed tofu is popular for stir-fries.

Clockwise from the top left: Firm tofu, Soft tofu, Smoked tofu, Silken tofu

TOFU TYPE	KEY CHARACTERISTICS	PREPARATION	IDEAL DISHES
Dried tofu	Fragile twists of custard-coloured dried tofu have a more intense flavour than fresh tofu. They are paper-thin and brittle and come in sheets, sticks or knots. Sometimes called 'beancurd sheets', 'tofu skin' or 'tofu pastry'. Found in large packets in the dried soup ingredients section of Asian stores. Most popular in Chinese cuisine.	Requires soaking for at least one hour before cooking, submerged completely in water. If the pieces need cutting down to size, use kitchen scissors rather than a knife, for better control.	Hotpots, stews, soups Pan-fries Desserts
Deep-fried tofu	Popular in Chinese and Japanese cuisine. There are two types: chunky cubes known as *atsuage*; or smaller thin pockets of deep-fried tofu for stuffing, known as *aburaage*. These are usually found in the chilled or frozen section of Asian stores.	Not essential, but a quick soak in hot water before cooking makes this type of tofu more porous and ready to take on new flavours.	Stir-fries Pan-fries For stuffing Slice and add to soups
Fermented tofu	Housed in charming ceramic or glass jars, small cubes of feta-like tofu are suspended in a brine. they have strong cheese, spice or wine flavours.	Simply remove the cubes from the jar, leaving the brine behind. Break the cubes down with a spoon to form a smooth paste before adding to cooking.	Marinades Stews Sauces
Sesame tofu	Not technically a tofu, this is sesame paste that has been set to achieve a tofu-like appearance and texture.	Simply serve as it is.	Dips Spreads

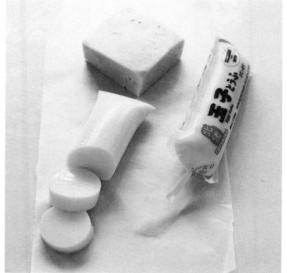

Clockwise from the top left: Dried tofu, Deep-fried
tofu, Silken and Egg tofu, Fermented tofu

A BRIEF HISTORY

Soya beans have been growing in China for more than three millennia. They are the foundation of so many Asian flavours and ingredients that we are familiar with today, from soy sauce to hoisin sauce, Japanese miso paste to Korean gochujang, fermented black beans to – of course – tofu. Soya and its many products have played a central role in Asian diets for centuries.

One of my earliest memories is being handed a warm bottle of soya milk by my grandma, when we visited her in Hong Kong (China). My grandparents ran a small home-made soya milk business in the city, making it fresh each morning and selling it on a stall to busy commuters. I would bet that I ate soya every single day of my childhood, whether it was as tofu, as soya milk or in a sauce. Tofu was often cooked with meat, fish or seafood too, so it was certainly not seen as a vegetarian dish; instead, it added texture, flavour and nutrition to all our meals.

In the West, tofu has long been considered to be a sad substitute for meat, often chosen for its stark nutritional qualities rather than any desire for culinary pleasure, which is a real shame. In its simplest form it is indeed quite plain in flavour… but then so is ricotta, or rice, or pasta; all these ingredients require great recipes to bring them to life.

Across East Asia, tofu is traditionally sold in family-run tofu shops that offer fresh-pressed tofu every morning, sold by weight and wrapped in cloths and boxes that are designed to be re-used each time a customer returns for more. Increasingly, these small businesses are dying out, as cities embrace supermarkets, which offer convenience and variety all under one roof. Here, boxes of pre-packed tofu are available and can be kept at home in the refrigerator for many days, or even weeks. Outside Asia, tofu was originally an ingredient that could only be found in health food shops, but in recent years, it is becoming a well-established subset of grocery, along with many other vegan and vegetarian ingredients, intended to help support the choices of a growing army of plant-based consumers.

While tofu is commonplace across all East Asia, how it is prepared does vary from country to country. In Japan, the dishes are generally light and celebrate the clean smoothness of tofu with minimal seasoning. In Korean food, tofu appears most often in spicy stews and soups. In Thai and Filipino cooking, it is often deep-fried before being added to dishes. It is in Chinese cooking where the types and usage of tofu are most varied: smoked tofu stir-fries are popular in Hunan; spicy braised tofu dishes in Sichuan; mashed and steamed tofu dishes with seafood in Canton. It is added to soups and braised in stews all across China, while dried tofu is found in Cantonese desserts as well as in savoury hotpots. Fermented tofu is most common in sauces and dips across Malaysia, China and other South East Asian countries.

In recent years, tofu is being used in really inventive dessert-making in Asia and beyond, where it is a lighter alternative to creamy puddings and forms a delicate backdrop to bolder flavours. We are used to seeing tofu paired with Asian ingredients such as ginger and miso, but it's amazing to see it today in Western recipes alongside the likes of vanilla, chocolate and caramel, too.

As a lifelong champion of tofu, it is wonderful for me to see it being embraced in everyday home cooking around the world. I hope this is just the beginning of more inventive ways of cooking with tofu, exploring it beyond the delicious classics of salt and pepper tofu, or ma po tofu.

小田原揚 ￥190

玉ネギ揚

たわら揚 ￥63円

ごぼう揚 ￥84円

ゼンマイ揚 ￥98円

椎茸揚 ￥115円

銀杏揚 ￥100円

百合根揚 ￥210円

納豆揚 ￥137円

枝豆揚 ￥100円

梅がんも ￥100

イカ揚 ￥137円

中華揚 ￥100円

エビ ￥137円

COOKING TIPS

For the uninitiated, tofu can be quite daunting to cook with, given its unfamiliar texture. But in fact it's simple to master tofu, once armed with a few tricks.

KEEPING TOFU FRESH

In countries where tofu shops are commonplace, such as China, Japan and Korea, tofu is sold by weight, deli-style, from buckets. The tofu will have been freshly made that morning – it's the freshest tofu you can buy – and is expected to be sold and eaten on the same day. It should always be kept in the refrigerator, to maintain its freshness.

Once you have opened a package of fresh tofu, any excess should be immersed in water, kept in the refrigerator and eaten within two or three days, changing the water daily to maintain freshness. If the tofu starts to turn a yellow colour, you should discard it. You need to refresh the water regularly, as otherwise the beany liquid that is expelled from the tofu will turn stale and the tofu itself will dry out and lose its fresh flavour. Alternatively, drain all the water out and seal in an airtight container or zip-lock bag and consume within 2 days.

Tofu that is sold from a store's ambient shelves in a cardboard carton, without a tray of liquid, is a reliable storecupboard staple. Once opened, keep it in the refrigerator and eat it within two days.

The key to a great tofu dish is to enjoy it at its freshest, so if you have any left over tofu, do try to use it up within a few days, or consider making a bigger batch of whatever you're making and freezing the excess.

Tofu freezes well, although the texture does alter. However, I don't recommend cooking it from frozen. During the freezing process, the porous tofu will form water crystals in its cavities and, if you cook it from frozen, this water will give you a watery dish. So after freezing tofu, defrost it thoroughly, leaving it to drain wrapped in kitchen paper (paper towels) to remove excess water.

DRAINING FRESH TOFU

Fresh tofu is normally sold in a tray of water that keeps it moist and fresh, but usually you do not want all that extra liquid in the finished dish. So, for all dishes using fresh tofu, draining is required. Simply place the tofu in a fine-meshed sieve over a sink to drain off the excess water. Depending on the type of tofu, this could take up to forty minutes. If the tofu needs pressing further for your dish after draining, see below.

PRESSING FRESH TOFU

Pressing tofu is a bit of pain, I admit, and I rarely do it. However, not all tofu – nor all tofu dishes – require pressing. For the recipes in this book, I always state whether the tofu needs draining and/or pressing. Pressing the tofu both intensifies the flavour, by removing excess water, and firms up the texture, which is essential for certain recipes such as burger patties and baked dishes. There are many dishes where it makes no difference if you press it or not, such as ma po tofu, soups, stews or desserts. Silken tofu, fermented and dried tofu never require pressing.

There are many gadgets you can buy that will help you press your tofu. However, my method is very simple and requires no special bits of equipment, just two trays or plates, kitchen paper (paper towels) and a weight such as a couple of cans of tomatoes or a heavy-based saucepan.

PRESSING FRESH TOFU: A STEP-BY-STEP GUIDE

1. Wrap the tofu in kitchen paper (paper towels)

2. Place in a large bowl, or on a tray or large plate with a lip, so that the water does not run out all over the kitchen.

3. Place another tray, large plate or wooden board on top and then a weight, such as two cans of tomatoes, a heavy-based saucepan or a heavy stone making sure the weight is evenly distributed across the tofu block.

4. Leave for at least thirty minutes and up to one hour, to press out the water.

5. When ready to use the tofu, remove the weight, tray and kitchen paper.

6. Wipe the tofu and it is ready to use. If the tofu needs to be firmer still, press it for longer, or use a heavier weight, again ensuring to distribute the weight evenly across the block.

BLANCHING TOFU

A quick dip in hot, salted water helps to wake up tofu's sweet beany flavours; this little trick is very worthwhile, especially if the tofu is not super-fresh. The quick flash of boiling heat forces more pores into the tofu as well, so can help it take on flavours more readily.

MICROWAVING FRESH TOFU

This is a trick that was taught to me recently by Malcolm, one of the founders of Miso Tasty. If you are short of time to press your tofu, a quick one-minute blast in the microwave on medium heat for a 300g/10½oz block will expel water and firm it up instantly. The proteins in the tofu will tighten, giving it a heavier, rubbery texture. It's great for dishes where a firmer texture is needed, such as dumpling fillings, burger patties or baked tofu steaks. This is a tofu hack to keep up your sleeve for when you are short on time, or you simply cannot be bothered to press it!

FREEZING TOFU

Freezing tofu changes its texture; the water crystals that form in its pores make a network of holes which, once thawed, creates a chewy texture. In some soup, stew or stir-fry dishes where you want this chewier texture, frozen tofu is perfect. Freezing it also means you always have tofu on hand for last-minute cooking, too.

CRISPING FRESH TOFU

There are a number of ways you can crisp up fresh tofu, including baking it, or dipping it into a batter before frying, but the easiest and most common way is to coat it lightly in flour before shallow frying. I find that a mix of flours creates the most satisfying crunch, but most flours work fine. My favourite is a half-and-half blend of cornflour (corn starch) and plain flour (all-purpose flour).

The key is for your oil to be nice and hot before the tofu hits the pan, and to have kitchen paper (paper towels) ready to receive the tofu once it is crispy all over, to blot off the excess oil. Take care to control the heat of the oil, especially if you are cooking a large batch. Oil that is not hot enough means you will struggle to achieve super-crispy pieces, but oil that is too hot will burn the flour coating easily. To avoid either of these scenarios, add tofu pieces to the oil one at a time, and in a clockwise formation, so you can keep track of when to turn each. If the tofu starts to turn a caramel colour straight away, it is time to reduce the heat; the tofu should crisp up without any colour to start with, and only turn golden after about one minute.

REHYDRATING DRIED TOFU

Dried tofu can take anything from ten minutes to one hour to rehydrate. It is important to soak it in warm or cold water, but never hot water, as that begins to expel some of the delicious flavour of the tofu too soon, before cooking. Submerge the tofu pieces completely in water; you will know they are fully rehydrated when they have turned a pale yellow colour, are plump and soft and tear easily if you pull them with your fingers. If they do not tear easily, they need to soak for a little longer, or the tofu will be too chewy in the finished dish. It is possible to over-soak dried tofu, so try to avoid soaking it for more than about six hours, or the pieces may fall apart when cooked. Once the soaking process is complete, leave the tofu pieces to drain in a sieve before using.

CUTTING TOFU

Fresh tofu is very easy to handle and can be lifted by hand and cut into slices or cubes simply with a sharp knife and a chopping board. Drained and pressed tofu is much easier to slice; the firmer texture supports a cleaner cut. Many stir-fried and pan-fried dishes call for cubes of tofu, and cutting to 1.5–2cm (around ¾ inch) thick is ideal. This can be tricky, since most tofu comes in rectangular blocks, but a good tip is to slice the tofu slab horizontally through its centre first – as if you were slicing a burger bun – before cutting it into cubes, first cutting lengthways, then widthways.

Silken tofu is the most challenging type of tofu to cut, since it is the most fragile. It usually comes in a cardboard carton, from which you need to carefully slide the block out onto a plate, or in a tube from which you need to carefully squeeze it out slowly, like toothpaste. For silken tofu blocks, if you need to slice them, cutting them into slabs no smaller than 2cm (¾ inch) is recommended, to keep the pieces robust for cooking; smaller bits will be difficult to handle. For tubes of egg tofu, use a pair of kitchen scissors to slice off medallions of tofu as you edge it out of the tube.

Dried tofu pieces are brittle and must be handled gently, but, once hydrated, they are pretty robust and elastic and are best cut with a sharp pair of kitchen scissors.

TOFU & HEALTH

Despite its innocent appearance, tofu packs a nutritional punch, so whatever diet or lifestyle you are following, tofu can find a place in it. Tofu has been a cornerstone for vegetarian diets in the West for decades, so it is fantastic to see it finally being embraced by non-vegetarians too, those looking to reduce their meat consumption as well as adventurous cooks keen to try out new ingredients.

Tofu's health profile is full of happy contradictions. Its light texture conceals a rich protein content: it is a complete protein and has higher protein levels than any other plant food, containing all eight of the amino acids that are essential for health. Even with its creamy texture and flavour, tofu is actually very low in calories and in saturated fats. Plus it is easy to digest and comforting to eat, making it perfect for all ages. In Asia, tofu is one of the first high-protein foods that babies try, as well as being a welcome comfort for the dentally challenged later in life!

A 150g/5½oz portion of firm tofu contains more than 20g/¾oz of protein, and it has been proven that consuming at least 25g/1oz of soya-based protein each day reduces blood cholesterol[1]. The impact of eating soya regularly is also related to the reduction of heart disease[2]. Most of the dishes in this book recommend a tofu portion size per person of about 150g/5½oz when it is a main course, but if you are eating it as part of a spread of dishes, 100g/3½oz per person is plenty. Tofu is deceptively filling, despite being pretty light, due to its satisfying high-protein levels.

At the same time, there has been a lot of scientific analysis and media attention on the health and ethics of eating soya-based foods, especially around the topics of genetic modification and on its impact on hormonal balance in humans. Many of the concerns are attributed to the isoflavones present in soya beans, a class of phytoestrogens that are similar to the oestrogen hormone. An in-depth analysis of the effects of soya on human health[3] acknowledged there was no evidence that populations which regularly eat high levels of soya – such as the Chinese and Japanese – have suffered a negative impact on their hormonal balance, or on related issues such as fertility. Nonetheless, soya remains a controversial topic for some, although the growing availability of organic, certified non-genetically modified tofu in health food shops and supermarkets has helped to overcome negative preconceptions.

As flexitarian, vegetarian and vegan diets continue to be on the rise, plant-based protein sources such as tofu and tempeh are being embraced with much less stigma than they were in the past. Lifestyles that are kinder both on the planet and to the body are key today, so the future for tofu is getting ever brighter.

[1] The UK government's Joint Claims Institute, 2002
[2] Mannu et al., 2013
[3] The UK Committee on Toxicity of Chemicals in Food Consumer Products and the Environment (COT, 2003)

MAKING TOFU FROM SCRATCH

To make your own tofu, you must first make soya milk.

Soya beans are soaked and puréed, then strained. This produces a thick, creamy-coloured liquid: soya milk. The milk is then cooked, to make it edible.

Soya milk is transformed into tofu with the help of a coagulant. In Japanese tofu, the natural coagulant (*nigari*) of magnesium chloride is usually used, while in China gypsum salts are more common. Sometimes acids – such as rice vinegar or lemon juice – can be employed. However, they all do the same job. Soft, satiny curds start to form, which are scooped out and pressed to form tofu pieces. The tofu is then covered in cold water to store.

If you don't wish to prepare tofu from the bean, it can be made from a regular bottle of soya milk instead. This will slash the preparation work by about half, and it is a great place to start if you have never made tofu before. However, making the tofu from scratch, using soya beans, will create a much purer flavour, as many industrially made soya milks have a lot of added water, making it harder to set the tofu firm and giving a less rich flavour.

HOME-MADE TOFU

This recipe makes soft or firm tofu, depending on the amount of weight you press it under. It is best enjoyed within four days of making. *Nigari* is easily available online.

Makes about 600g/1lb 5oz

800g/1lb 12oz/4 cups dried soya beans

1½ tsp natural nigari flakes, plus another 1 tsp if needed

Equipment

high-powered blender or food processor

large colander

muslin or cheesecloth

trivet that fits the colander

1. First, pick over the soya beans and discard any that are a little darker; you're looking for uniformity in colour. Wash them in three changes of water, then drain. Soak the beans in 1.5 litres/2½ pints of soft filtered water for 10 hours, then wash and drain them for a final time.

2. Next is the purée stage; the soya beans need to be puréed with 1 litre/1¾ pints of warm water in a high-powered blender, or a food processor fitted with a fine blade. With this amount, it is best to do it across a few batches. You need to blend each batch for a few minutes until it becomes a smooth purée. You should have about 2 litres/3½ pints of puréed soya beans.

3. Line a colander with a piece of muslin or cheesecloth, leaving enough material to overhang the sides by a good way, as you will be making it into a bag later. Place the colander in a large bowl. Bring 2 litres/3½ pints of water to the boil in a large saucepan. Pour in all the bean purée and stir, then pour the contents of the saucepan into your muslin-lined colander.

4. Close the top of the muslin and seal it with string. Using the bottom of a jar or a rolling pin for assistance, push as much soya milk out as you can (avoid touching the hot bag of soya with your hands). This gets easier as the mixture cools, when you can start to use your hands to squeeze out any remaining milk.

pan, reduce the heat and allow it to simmer for 10 minutes.

6. Meanwhile, put 1½ tsp of the nigari flakes in a small bowl and dissolve them with 5 tbsp of warm water.

7. Now is the fiddly bit. Place the cleaned large colander in the sink and place inside a trivet, such as you might use for steaming. It should have small holes and be a circular shape that fits inside the colander. My trivet is about 18cm/7 inches in diameter and fits about two-thirds of the way down the colander. Finally, spread a muslin or cheesecloth, folded to roughly a 40cm/16 inch square, over the trivet, and allow the edges to hang over the sides of the colander.

8. Once the soya milk has simmered for 10 minutes, take it off the heat and carefully add the nigari solution to it in a spiral motion, to ensure that it is evenly distributed in the milk, starting from the outside in. Now cover the pot for 10–12 minutes while the curds form.

9. The curds will separate from the watery, greenish whey. If curds do not form, you will need to go through the process again: reheat the soya milk and create a new nigari solution, using 1 tsp of nigari and 2 tbsp of warm water. Gently stir it in again, remove from the heat and cover for a further 10 minutes. The curds should fully form.

5. Clean the large saucepan and pour the strained soya milk into it. Bring the milk to the boil, taking care as it can bubble up quickly. As soon as the soya milk begins to rise up in the

12. Finally, fill a large bowl of water with at least 15cm/6 inches of cold water. Lift up the tofu curds – they will now have formed a solid cake – from the colander, using the muslin, and gently slide into the bowl of water. Carefully remove the muslin while the tofu is submerged.

10. Now pour the curds and whey into the colander in the sink and lift up the overhanging cheesecloth to cover the top. Find a weight that is the closest fit to the top of the curds; a plate and a couple of cans of beans are good, or a saucepan with the right-sized base. The weight should be about 650g/1lb 7oz for medium-firm tofu.

13. The tofu is now edible, ready to be used in any number of dishes. Its texture should be medium-firm. Very fresh tofu tends to be more fragile, so if you plan to use it in a stir-fry, I recommend pressing it for at least 30 minutes first. Keep the tofu refrigerated in a water bath for up to 4 days, changing the water every day. If you don't refresh the water, the beany liquid that leaches out of the tofu will turn stale and the tofu itself will dry out more rapidly and lose its fresh flavour. This applies equally to shop-bought tofu.

11. If you have a tofu press, this usually has a wooden block on top, upon which you add the weights. Try to make sure the weight is placed in the centre. Leave the curds to be pressed for at least 20 minutes.

HOT-SMOKED BARBECUE TOFU

A great addition to a summer barbecue spread, or an excuse to get the barbecue out during cooler months, this smoked tofu has a deep, sweet smoked flavour that permeates it throughout. Smoked tofu is a popular stir-fry ingredient in a number of regional Chinese cuisines, and this is a cooking method that is well-suited to its firm texture. It makes a great protein-rich topping for a salad and a satisfying sandwich or burger filling too; just add tomatoes, a spicy relish, pickles and a soft bread bun.

Makes 400g/14oz

400g/14oz pressed firm tofu
3 tbsp toasted sesame oil

Equipment

handful of smoking chips
foil
barbecue with lid
charcoal

1. First get the wood chips ready. Put them in a bowl of room-temperature water and leave them for 90 minutes. Next press the firm tofu, to remove any excess water, or buy ready-pressed tofu.

2. To get the barbecue ready, make a tray to hold water using foil, it should be larger than the slab of tofu, with sides at least 2.5cm/1 inch high. Place the tray on the barbecue bed where the charcoal goes in. Pile up the charcoal next to it and light it.

3. Once the tofu has been pressed, slice it into chunky strips, or whatever shape you plan to use in your cooking. I like to keep it as a whole slab, but you may want it in chunks. Brush on all sides with sesame oil.

4. Once the barbecue has slowed down to a glow and there are no more flames, you are ready to smoke the tofu. Fill the foil tray you made with water and scatter just 3–4 wood chips over the hot coals. Now put the lid on the barbecue, but make sure the vent is across the part where the tofu will be placed and open, to allow the smoke to be pulled past the tofu, thereby smoking it. You are looking for a gentle dribble of smoke out of the barbecue and not a strong current, so adjust the vents accordingly. Maintain this for 10–15 minutes.

5. Finally, open the barbecue, put the tofu on the grill directly over the water bath and close the lid again. Keep an eye on the heat and make sure there is a gentle trickle of smoke coming out of the barbecue; add more charcoal if it is burning out and add more wood chips when the smoke slows down. If the water bath dries out, top it up.

6. After 45–50 minutes, turn the tofu pieces over, close the lid again and leave for a final 30 minutes. The tofu should be a beautiful charred dark brown colour. Leave to cool before using.

CHINESE SPICY FERMENTED TOFU

Foo Yee

I usually buy jars of Chinese fermented tofu from the Asian store, but I have experimented with making my own too, which has a milder taste and uses only natural preservatives. My recipe is inspired by Sichuan flavours, but you can swap the Sichuan pepper for regular chilli flakes as well. Beware, if you share your kitchen with anyone else: a warning to them of the incoming distinctive aroma would be a kind gesture.

Makes 450g/1lb

For the tofu

1 litre/1¾ pints/4½ cups filtered water

1 tsp fine sea salt

450g/1lb block of firm tofu, halved

2 heaped tbsp Sichuan peppercorns, ground

For the brine

375ml/13fl oz/1½ cups filtered water

3 tbsp fine sea salt

1 tbsp caster sugar (superfine sugar)

120ml/4fl oz/½ cup Shaoxing rice wine

Equipment

disposable gloves

glass jar with a rubber seal

1. As with all fermenting, hygiene is very important, so I recommend wearing disposable gloves for handling the tofu. You also need to sterilize a jar. To do so:

2. Preheat the oven to 160°C fan/ 180°C/350°F/gas mark 4 for 20 minutes. Meanwhile, wash the jars and lids in hot soapy water and leave them to drain for 10 minutes, but don't dry them with a cloth. Place the jar standing upright on a baking tray and bake for 10 minutes. Place the lid in a large bowl and pour boiling water on to cover. Leave to soak for 10 minutes. Once the jar and lid have cooled, they are ready to use.

3. In a medium-sized pan, boil the measured water with the salt. Once on a rolling boil, add the tofu pieces and boil for 5 minutes. This encourages the tofu to be more porous, which will help it to take on flavour from the brine.

4. Lay out a couple of pieces of kitchen paper (paper towels). Remove the tofu from the water with a slotted spoon and place it on the kitchen paper, layer more kitchen paper over, then top with a heavy chopping board or tray. Add weights, such as a few cans of tomatoes or a heavy pan, to squeeze out any excess water. Leave for at least 4 hours, but ideally overnight.

5. On a clean chopping board, cut the tofu into 2.5cm/1 inch cubes and place them on a kitchen paper-lined tray or plate, leaving 2.5cm/1 inch gaps between each cube. Add another layer of kitchen paper on top, then wrap the whole plate or tray with clingfilm (plastic wrap) so it is airtight. This protects the tofu while it starts to ferment. Place the tray of tofu in a dark place at around 25°C/77°F and let it ferment for 2–3 days. If your kitchen is warmer than this, it will take a shorter time to start. The tofu will take on a light orange colour and start to emit a rather pungent smell! If you spot white mould on it, don't worry, but if the mould is any other colour, simply scrape it off.

6. Next make the brine. Boil the measured water with the salt and sugar for 2 minutes, and then add the rice wine.

7. Open up the fermenting tofu and, one by one, coat each piece on all sides with the Sichuan pepper before placing it inside the sterilized glass jar. Once you have filled the jar, pour the brine on top to completely cover the tofu. Seal the jar and leave in a cool, dark place at around 20°C/68°F for a minimum of 4 weeks. You will see that the tofu starts to get stronger and darker in colour.

8. Enjoy as a dip, stir-fry sauce, marinade, or in a hotpot (see pages 108–117).

JAPANESE DEEP-FRIED TOFU

Atsuage

Deep-fried tofu can be found in the chilled and frozen sections of Asian stores and is usually of fantastic quality. *Aburaage*, which are little pockets of tofu skins ready for stuffing with rice or slicing into light soups (see pages 124–125), are really worth buying from specialist stores.

However, *atsuage*, or 'tofu puffs', are much chunkier and can vary in quality when bought, depending on their freshness, so I much prefer to make these myself. These are great added to soups, stews, and stir-fries (see page 125).

Makes 600g/1lb 5oz

600g/1lb 5oz firm fresh tofu, drained and pressed (see pages 14–15)

800ml/1½ pints/3¼ cups sunflower oil, for deep-frying

1. Slice the pressed tofu into 8–10 large chunks, depending on the dish you plan to use them in.

2. Heat the sunflower oil in a deep saucepan to 180°C/350°F, or until a cube of bread browns in 30 seconds; the oil should be at least 7.5cm/ 3 inches deep and come no more than one-third of the way up the sides of the pan. As always when deep-frying, be very careful and do not leave the kitchen.

3. Using a slotted spoon, place 2 tofu pieces into the oil. It will spit a little, so take care as you turn the tofu to get a golden colour all over. Lift out with the slotted spoon onto kitchen paper (paper towels) once the pieces are golden brown and puffy. Repeat to fry the remaining tofu.

4. Once cooled, the tofu puffs can be refrigerated in an airtight container to keep them fresh, but eat them within 2 days. Tofu puffs do not freeze well, as the air pockets from the frying collapse, causing it to lose all the chewy deliciousness that you have created.

5. Before adding the tofu puffs to dishes, refresh them quickly by dunking them into boiling water for a few seconds; this makes them more porous, supple and ready to take on new flavours.

TOFU CHEESE
Tofu Misozuke

This Japanese delicacy hails from Fukuoka. It is essentially a miso-fermented tofu that can be enjoyed as an umami-rich spread or dip. Thinned down with olive oil, it can also be used as a sauce or dressing, or a medium in which to stir-fry vegetables. Creamy and tangy, it is often thought of as a naturally vegan cheese alternative, that is made from only two ingredients. There's an eight-week waiting time, and some maintenance every few days, but it is well worth it! I first tried this in a Japanese fermented food restaurant in Tokyo and I couldn't stop thinking about it afterwards. I had to make my own!

Tofu misozuke is delicious on crackers or toast, in a banh mi (see page 116) or as a dip with vegetable crudités. Adding fresh herbs before serving really lifts its flavours; chives and parsley work particularly well.

Makes 400g/14oz

400g/14oz block of firm tofu, drained and pressed (see pages 14–15)

300g/10½oz/1 generous cup unpasteurized white miso paste

Equipment

Glass container with lid

1. Wrap the pressed tofu in kitchen paper (paper towels) and set aside for 30 minutes, to absorb any final drops of liquid.

2. Using a spatula or butter knife, spread the miso paste all over the tofu, in a layer about 1cm/½ inch thick. Make sure it is a complete layer with no gaps, as any exposed tofu will develop mould.

3. Place the wrapped tofu in a sterilized (see page 25) airtight glass container, seal it and put it in the refrigerator for 8 weeks.

4. Every 2–3 days, the liquid that pools in the bottom of the container will need to be drained away, or the tofu will turn mouldy. Also wipe down the lid if there is any condensation.

5. After 8 weeks, discard the miso (scrape it off with a spatula or table knife, or just use your fingers) and the tofu is ready to eat.

6. This will keep for up to 2 months, stored in a glass container lined with kitchen paper, which needs changing every few days for freshness.

TWISTS

For a stronger flavour, try red or barley miso instead of white miso.

DASHI

Vegetarian Japanese stock is great to have on hand for enhancing many of the dishes in this book. It is a great swap in Asian food for classic vegetable stock for many reasons, but mostly because vegetable stock is based on a French mirepoix of ingredients, including quite distinctive flavours such as garlic and celery, which in some more subtle dishes – including miso soup – are too intrusive. There is also the advantage of not having added salt, which is in most instant vegetable stocks, so you can better control the seasoning of your dish.

There are a few ways to make dashi, but the most common uses kombu, a Japanese kelp. You can buy packs of dried powdered *kombudashi* from Asian stores or online; I always have packets at home if I don't have time to make dashi. If you want to try the original fish-based Japanese dashi, which has a smokier flavour, search for *katsuobushi* instead.

Dashi making is not at all complicated, no more difficult than making a coffee in a press or tea in a teapot. My recipe includes shiitake mushrooms for a deeper, sweeter flavour and increased umami levels.

Makes 1 litre/1¾ pints/4¼ cups

10g/¼oz kombu (dried kelp)

1 litre/1¾ pints/4 cups filtered or soft water

30g/1oz dried shiitake mushrooms

1. Kombu comes in large sheets that require cutting down to size. Once you have weighed the amount of kombu that you need, I recommend that you make some extra cuts into the pieces with scissors to increase the surface area and help the flavour to release into the water.

2. Pour the measured filtered water into a large bowl or saucepan and add the kombu and shiitake mushrooms. Cover with clingfilm (plastic wrap) or a lid and leave for at least 2 hours or overnight.

3. Pour the mixture into a saucepan, if it is not already in one, and remove the mushrooms. Simmer over a medium-low heat until just before boiling, then remove the kombu. It is really important that you don't boil the kombu, or it loses its delicate flavours. My friend Tim Anderson, of Nanban Japanese restaurant

in London, recommends toasting kombu over an open flame for a deeper flavour before soaking it.

4. The dashi can be kept in the refrigerator, covered, or in a closed bottle, for 3 days, or in the freezer for up to 2 months.

5. To make *katsuobushi*, which is more common in Japanese cooking and includes dried, smoked fish, follow the steps above, but add 10g/¼oz katsuobushi (dried bonito flakes) as soon as the saucepan has been taken off the heat. Allow it to steep in the dashi for 5 minutes, then return the pan to the heat and simmer for 4 minutes. Finally, strain the dashi by placing 2 sheets of kitchen paper (paper towels) in a fine-meshed sieve and pouring the dashi through it. Use immediately, or bottle and refrigerate for up to 3 days, or freeze for up to 1 month.

BAO

If you cannot get hold of bao at your supermarket or Asian store, then you can make your own. It is not as tricky as you might think, but you do need to manage the timings well, as the dough needs to prove twice before it goes into the steamer.

Makes 12 large buns

100ml/3½fl oz/½ cup oat milk or regular whole milk

90ml/6 tbsp warm water

1½ tsp instant or fast-action dried yeast

2 tbsp vegetable oil, plus extra for greasing

350g/12oz/3 cups plain flour (all-purpose flour), plus extra for dusting

2 tsp baking powder

1 tbsp caster sugar (superfine sugar)

1. In a medium-sized bowl, mix together the milk, warm water, yeast and oil and leave it for 10 minutes to check that the yeast bubbles up to create a foamy top. This will tell you if your yeast is working or not.

2. Put all the remaining ingredients in a large mixing bowl and mix together with a wooden spoon, then slowly pour in the liquid little by little until the dough begins to come together. Start using your hands to bring the dough together into a ball. If it gets a bit sticky, dust with a little extra flour so the ball of dough comes together off the bottom and sides of the bowl.

3. Now knead the dough for 10 minutes on a work surface, stretching and folding the dough.

4. Place the kneaded dough in a lightly oiled bowl, cover with clingfilm (plastic wrap) or a tea towel (dish towel) and leave for about 1 hour or until doubled in size. Once it has reached this stage, knock the dough back by kneading it for a further 2–3 minutes, then immediately cut it into 12 even portions. Cover with a tea towel.

5. Cut 12 x 10cm/4 inch squares of non-stick baking paper (parchment paper).

6. Using a rolling pin, roll each ball of dough into an oval shape, roughly 15cm/6 inches long and 7.5cm/3 inches wide. Fold in half widthways to create a bao. To stop the bao from sticking together, brush with a little oil on the inside and on the top before placing it on a square of baking paper. Repeat this for as many baos as you can fit into your steamer, then add them all to a steamer basket (cold, not over the heat), and cover.

7. Leave the baos to prove a second time inside the basket for another 30–60 minutes, or until they have risen again.

8. Prepare the hot water for your steamer and steam the bao for 8 minutes, or until puffy and firm.

9. These are great for freezing once steamed, if you have excess. Once steamed, it is best to eat them within a day to enjoy them completely fresh, as they do turn stale quite quickly.

CRISPY TOFU

I didn't mean to kick off this book with the nutritionally naughtiest of tofu dishes, but for the uninitiated, crispy tofu really is the place to begin.

Crisping up the edges of tofu performs three major jobs. The first is to create textural contrast, as the hard crunch gives way to a soft melting middle; the second is to protect the natural juiciness of tofu with an extra casing; the last is to add a sharp contrast of flavour with every seasoned bite.

The best crispy tofu starts with tofu that has very little moisture, so always drain and press it (see pages 14–15) for at least 20 minutes before cooking; it should be compact and firm. Low moisture is key to achieving the crispiest edges, so it really is worth the extra effort. Pressing it makes it easier to handle in the pan, too.

Start your tofu journey here with these total crowd-pleasers. They will pique your interest to explore deeper into the world of tofu.

OAT FLAKE SALT & PEPPER TOFU

An absolute classic; the combination of salt and pepper is delightful. Creamy tofu calms the dish down, while the sharp seasoning teases the palate. This dish is all about chasing that salty, tantalizing heat, down to the final bits of charred onion. Oat flakes provide my killer twist; plump and ready to take on the magic dust, they add that extra nuggetty chew, allowing the punchy flavours to linger for longer and the tofu to shine even more brightly. Here I take on the challenge of pushing this already 'A' dish to an 'A star'… and I dare you to leave a single morsel behind.

Serves 2 as a main course, or 4 as a starter or side dish

300g/10½oz firm tofu, drained for 20 minutes and sliced into 1.5cm/½ inch cubes

100g/3½oz/¾ cup cornflour (corn starch)

6 tbsp vegetable oil, plus extra if needed

2 tsp sea salt flakes

1 tsp freshly fine-ground black pepper

1 large chilli, deseeded and finely sliced, plus extra to serve

2 spring onions (scallions), finely sliced, plus extra to serve

4–5 tbsp jumbo rolled oats

leaves from 2 coriander (cilantro) sprigs

greens or salad, and rice, to serve (optional)

1. Put the tofu cubes in a shallow dish with the cornflour and turn them gently, to coat all sides.

2. Heat half the oil in a large frying pan (skillet) over a high heat until bubbling hot, then add the cubes one by one, making sure there is at least 1cm/½ inch between each cube. (You may need to do this in batches.) If you need more oil to fry all the tofu, add a little more. Turn the cubes until all sides are crisp and golden. Drain on kitchen paper (paper towels).

3. In a small bowl, mix the salt and pepper together.

4. In a clean frying pan, heat up the remaining oil for 2 minutes, then add the chilli and spring onions. Stir-fry for 2 minutes, then add the oats and sprinkle with the salt and pepper. Stir-fry gently for a further 2 minutes, until the oats are golden and have taken on the flavours.

5. Add the crispy tofu, tossing it in the pan until the seasonings coat the cubes. Serve immediately, scattered with more chilli and spring onion and the coriander. Just as it is, this is a great starter; add greens or salad and rice if you are eating it as a main course.

TWISTS

This recipe is also great with whole button mushrooms instead of tofu, or – which is the classic dish – with squid.

AGEDASHI TOFU

I would not dream of eating in an *izayaka* (Japanese pub) and not ordering this dish. For me, it is compulsory. Outside Japan, I still find excuses to order it, or, even better, to make it at home. Agedashi tofu is essentially a crispy deep-fried tofu, served in a seasoned soy-based sauce, with grated radish and toppings such as spring onions and bonito flakes. If you don't mind deep-frying at home, this is a quick and easy starter or side dish, and incredibly easy to get right.

Serves 4 as a starter

500ml/18fl oz/2 generous cups dashi (see pages 27–8)

5 tbsp light soy sauce

5 tbsp mirin

400g/14oz soft or silken tofu, drained for 20 minutes (see pages 14–15)

6 tbsp cornflour (corn starch)

vegetable oil, for deep-frying

2 spring onions (scallions), finely sliced

1 tbsp grated daikon (white radish), to serve (optional)

1. Prepare the sauce by mixing the dashi, soy sauce and mirin together in a bowl.

2. Next, slice the tofu into 4 x 100g/3½oz blocks and coat the pieces in the cornflour.

3. Fill a large saucepan or wok with enough oil to sit at least 2cm/¾ inch deep and heat it up for 3–4 minutes. As always when deep-frying, be very careful and do not leave the kitchen or take a telephone call.

4. Drop 2 of the tofu blocks into the oil; they should sizzle immediately. If they don't, the oil is not hot enough. Fry for 3–4 minutes until lightly golden brown, then lift out onto kitchen paper (paper towels) to drain off the excess oil. Fry the remaining 2 pieces in the same way before serving up into bowls.

5. Divide the sauce between the bowls, pouring it around the tofu, not on top of it.

6. Scatter with spring onions and grated daikon to serve.

TWISTS

Bonito fish flakes are a traditional topping for this classic dish, adding extra umami as well as providing a pretty pink crown for the tofu pieces.

BOOKSHOP KATSU

The mother of all comfort dishes. I first tried this on a particularly stressful day rushing around Tokyo, and it arrived as if sent from heaven. We stumbled across a tiny katsu curry booth within a station bookshop. The staff appeared like a mirage, offering us vegetable katsu curry with melted cheese on top. This recipe arrived in my hour of need, and I am sharing it in profound gratitude. You could say that the cheese is optional, but, for me, it is absolutely essential.

Serves 4

For the tofu

2 eggs, lightly beaten

100g/3½oz/1 cup panko crumbs

400g/14oz firm tofu, drained for 20 minutes, pressed (see pages 14–15) and cut into 2cm (¾ inch) rectangular slabs

vegetable oil, for frying

rice and vegetables, to serve

100g/3½oz/1 cup grated Cheddar, or other hard cheese

For the curry sauce

40ml/1½fl oz/3 tbsp vegetable oil

1 carrot, roughly chopped

1 large onion, roughly chopped

44g/1½oz/⅓ cup medium curry powder

85g/3oz/⅓ cup caster sugar (superfine sugar)

10g/¼oz/2 tsp sea salt flakes

15g/½oz/1 tbsp cornflour (corn starch)

2 tsp light soy sauce

200ml/7fl oz/¾ cup water

2½ tsp tomato purée (tomato paste)

2½ tsp white wine vinegar

pinch of cayenne pepper

1. First make the sauce. In a large, heavy-based saucepan, heat up the oil for a few minutes before adding the carrot and onion. Stir-fry over a medium heat for 3–4 minutes until the vegetables begin to soften. Add 3 tbsp water and put the lid on.

2. In a mixing bowl, mix the curry powder, sugar, salt, cornflour, soy sauce and measured water and mix until smooth. Add it to the pan of vegetables, stirring vigorously to stop any lumps. Then add the tomato purée, vinegar and cayenne.

3. Reduce the heat to low and simmer the sauce for 5–10 minutes. It will thicken as you cook.

4. Put the eggs for the tofu in a shallow dish and the panko in another. Dip the tofu in the egg, then press the slabs into the panko until covered and sticking on all sides.

5. Heat enough oil in a frying pan (skillet) to cover the base by 3mm/ ⅛ inch. Add the tofu and fry for 3–4 minutes on each side or until golden, turning carefully with tongs. Preheat the grill (broiler) to high.

6. When ready to serve, loosen up the curry sauce with 3–4 tbsp water, or until you are happy with the consistency. Distribute the tofu and sauce between ovenproof plates, sprinkle with the cheese, if using, and melt it under the hot grill (broiler). Serve with rice and vegetables.

TWISTS

You could also try different vegetables in the curry sauce, such as mushrooms or sweet potatoes. Instead of tofu, you could try chicken breast or white fish fillets.

TOFISH SEAWEED NUGGETS

These little matchbox-sized tofu nuggets, hugged around with toasted seaweed, are laced with the taste of the sea. Fried together in little bundles, they are totally irresistible, and fantastic washed down with beers or something bubbly. I often serve them with roasted potato wedges as a pleasing chippie alternative; add tartare or horseradish sauce as a dip for the full experience!

Serves 2 as a main course, or 4 as a side dish or starter

400g/14oz firm tofu, cut into 10–12 chunky matchbox-sized pieces, about 1cm/½ inch thick, drained

4–5 sheets nori

100ml/3½fl oz/scant ½ cup light soy sauce

2 garlic cloves, finely grated

sunflower oil, for deep-frying

100g/3½oz/¾ cup plain flour (all-purpose flour)

170ml/6fl oz/¾ cup ice-cold sparkling water

1. Wrap each piece of tofu with strips of nori seaweed of the same width, so that the tofu piece is completely covered. Arrange in a baking dish.

2. Make the marinade by mixing together the soy sauce and garlic. Pour the marinade over the tofu and rest in the refrigerator for 2 hours.

3. Heat enough oil for deep-frying in a large saucepan or wok. As always when deep-frying, be very careful and do not leave the kitchen or take a telephone call. The oil should come no more than one-third of the way up the sides of the pan.

4. In another bowl, mix together the flour and ice-cold water to make a batter.

5. Once the oil is hot enough at 170°C/340°F (a cube of bread will brown in 30 seconds), lift each piece of seaweed-wrapped tofu with tongs or chopsticks, dip into the batter, then deep-fry in the hot oil until golden brown, about 2 minutes on each side. Depending on how big your pan is, try not to fry more than 3 pieces at a time, or to crowd each piece too much.

6. Drain each piece on kitchen paper (paper towels). Great with tartare sauce or horseradish sauce, or simply ketchup!

TOFU & VEGETABLE TEMPURA

It is hard to resist ordering tempura at a restaurant: airy and light, the Japanese know how to deep-fry to a wafer-thin crisp. The key is to keep the batter super-light and cold, to avoid a heavy scampi-like coating. Tempura is great for vegetables and seafood that have a little moisture, and tofu works a treat in this mix; its creamy firmness loves the crispy white lacing and contrasts well against the savoury-sour dipping sauce.

Serves 4 as part of a sharing meal

For the tempura

2 small sweet potatoes, peeled
2 courgettes (zucchini)
250g/9oz firm tofu, drained and pressed (see pages 14–15)
200g/7oz/1½ cups plain flour (all-purpose flour), plus 2 tbsp
2 tbsp cornflour (corn starch), sifted
2 tsp baking powder
250ml/9fl oz/1 cup sunflower oil
20 ice cubes
1 large egg
240ml/9fl oz/1 cup ice-cold sparkling water

For the dipping sauce

3 tbsp light soy sauce
1 tsp toasted sesame oil
1 tbsp rice wine vinegar
1 tsp finely chopped thin spring onion (scallion) or coriander (cilantro) stem

TWISTS

Add some prawns (shrimp) or pieces of fish fillet to the mix of tempura, for more variety and textures.

1. Cut the vegetables and tofu into 5mm/¼ inch slices or into thick batons. It's great to vary the shape of each ingredient.

2. Get a few things ready ahead of the frying. Spread the 2 tbsp plain flour on a large plate. Get 2 large glass or metal bowls, one a little smaller than the other so you can nest the smaller bowl inside the larger one.

3. In a separate bowl, combine the cornflour and baking powder. In another bowl, combine the dipping sauce ingredients and set aside.

4. Pour the sunflower oil into a small saucepan and set it over a medium heat; the oil should come no higher than one-third of the sides of the pan. Allow it to reach 180°C/350°F, or until a cube of bread browns in 30 seconds.

5. Meanwhile, place the ice cubes in the large glass or metal bowl and rest the smaller bowl on top. Whisk the egg in the small bowl until frothy and then add the cold sparkling water.

6. Gradually mix in the cornflour mixture and the rest of the plain flour by hand. Don't overmix the batter or it will end up heavy. Don't worry if there are lumps, this is normal!

7. Using tongs or chopsticks, take each piece of vegetable and tofu and coat it in the 2 tbsp plain flour before immersing it in the cold batter.

8. Once the oil comes to temperature, test it by dropping some tempura batter in it. If it drops to the bottom but comes up straight away, the oil is hot enough. (If the vegetables do not drop to the bottom, the oil is too hot so adjust the heat.) Depending on the size of your pan and vegetables, fry 2–3 pieces at a time.

9. Cook the tempura for 1–2 minutes, depending on thickness and hardness (courgettes cook quicker than sweet potatoes, for example), then turn and cook for another 1–2 minutes – until both sides are lightly browned. Once they achieve the desired colour, take them out with a slotted spoon and place them on a piece of kitchen paper (paper towel) to drain any excess oil.

10. Serve straight after frying, with the dipping sauce on the side.

BLACK PEPPER BUTTER TOFU

This warming dish gives you all the heat you need without the spike of chilli. The dark and sticky soy butter flavours enhance the creamy sweetness of the tofu, while the peppery ginger heat arrives to balance it out just before the dish becomes too rich.

Wolf this down with copious amounts of rice, and greens such as spinach or broccoli.

Serves 2 as a main, or 4 as part of a sharing meal

- 300g/10½oz firm tofu, drained and cut into 1.5cm/½ inch thick rectangular pieces
- 100g/3½oz/¾ cup cornflour (corn starch)
- vegetable oil, for frying
- 6 spring onions (scallions), finely sliced
- 1 red onion, finely sliced
- ½ red pepper (bell pepper), finely sliced
- 1 garlic bulb, cloves separated and finely sliced
- 3 tbsp minced fresh ginger
- 100g/3½oz/1 stick unsalted butter
- 3 tbsp light soy sauce
- 4 tbsp dark soy sauce
- 2½ tbsp brown sugar
- 2–5 tbsp coarsely crushed black pepper, depending on how spicy you like it (use a mortar and pestle or spice grinder – it is worth it!)
- steamed rice, or plain noodles, to serve

1. First coat the tofu in the cornflour until all the sides are covered.

2. In a frying pan (skillet), heat 3 tbsp vegetable oil until bubbling hot and add the tofu pieces one by one, making sure there is at least 1cm/½ inch of space between each (split into separate batches if required and add more oil). Turn the tofu pieces until all sides are crunchy and golden. Drain on kitchen paper (paper towels).

3. Clean out the frying pan and heat up another 3 tbsp vegetable oil for 2 minutes before adding the red onion and spring onions, and stir-fry until softened.

4. Next add the red pepper, garlic and ginger to the pan, then the butter.

5. In a small bowl, mix the soy sauces and brown sugar, then add to the pan. Stir frequently to ensure the butter doesn't split from the sauce.

6. Finally add the black pepper to the pan, stir for 1 minute, then return the tofu and stir through gently to ensure it is covered with the sauce.

7. Serve immediately with steamed rice or plain noodles.

TWISTS

This sauce is highly addictive and fantastic on fish and chicken, too.

To make this dish vegan simply swap out the butter for 50ml/1¾fl oz/scant ¼ cup of vegetable oil.

PANKO TOFU BAO

These little pillow-soft wrapped tofu buns are the juicy burgers of East Asian street food. They are impressive to serve, but super-easy to make. Crispy breaded pieces of tofu, cosily tucked into a bun, drizzled with a bit of mayo and spicy tonkatsu sauce, this is a total crowd-pleaser. If you can't get hold of bao (though look in your local Asian store), it will also work with sweeter soft breads such as milk buns, brioche, or good old white sliced. If you have the time and patience, you can even make your own bao (see page 29).
All the effort here is in the prep, so you can serve the bao quickly and effortlessly.

Serves 4/Makes 8

For the bao

1 egg, lightly beaten

120g/4½oz/1¼ cups panko crumbs

400g/14oz firm tofu, drained for 20 minutes, pressed (see pages 14–15) and cut into 8 x 1.5cm/½ inch rectangular slabs

8 bao buns (see recipe introduction)

vegetable oil, for frying

8 Romaine lettuce leaves

8 cucumber slices

100ml/3½fl oz/scant ½ cup mayonnaise

70ml/2½fl oz/¼ cup brown sauce (optional)

8 small wooden skewers, or toothpicks

For the quick tonkatsu sauce (optional)

1 tbsp tomato ketchup

2½ tsp Worcestershire sauce

1½ tsp oyster sauce

1½ tsp caster sugar (superfine sugar)

1. If you are making your own tonkatsu sauce, mix all the ingredients in a bowl and set aside.

2. Put the egg for the bao in a shallow dish and the panko in another. Dip the tofu in the egg, then press the slabs into the panko until covered and sticking on all sides.

3. Prepare the bao buns by steaming them in a microwave with clingfilm (plastic wrap) on top, or, if using brioche buns, place in a preheated oven at 180°C fan/200°C/400°F/gas mark 6 for 4 minutes.

4. Heat up a large frying pan (skillet) over a high heat, filled with enough oil to cover the base by 1cm/½ inch. Fry the tofu slabs for 2–3 minutes on each side, or until golden.

5. Assemble the buns by filling them with the lettuce and cucumber. Spread the mayonnaise and tonkatsu sauce, or brown sauce, on the tofu pieces, then add them to the buns, holding them together with skewers or toothpicks. Serve immediately.

TWISTS

Instead of tonkatsu sauce, you can try tartare sauce, sriracha, hoisin or brown sauce, which can all be bought in most supermarkets.

TOFU MISO DENGAKU

The beany companionship of miso and tofu in this dish is wonderfully balanced. The Japanese *dengaku* technique is where tofu or vegetables are skewered like kebabs and grilled with a sweet miso sauce. It looks impressive and is great as a sharing dish, but if you are in a hurry, you can skip the skewer part and simply enjoy these tasty tofu dominos over a steaming bowl of rice.

The sauce is sweet and deeply savoury at the same time, and the recipe varies region by region. Darker miso, such as red miso, or hatcho miso from Nagoya, is most commonly used for this dish, but if you only have white miso or saikyo miso (from Kyoto) to hand, the recipe still works and gives a lighter, sweeter finish that is still incredible.

Serves 4

For the tofu

1 tbsp vegetable oil, plus extra for the baking tray

400g/14oz medium or soft tofu, drained and pressed (see pages 14–15)

1 tsp toasted sesame seeds

For the miso dengaku sauce

2 tbsp sake

2 tbsp mirin

2 tbsp caster sugar (superfine sugar), or 3 tbsp if using hatcho miso

4 tbsp red miso paste, or hatcho miso paste

1. Preheat the oven to 200°C fan/220°C/425°F/gas mark 7 and oil a baking tray.

2. Now make the sauce. Combine the sake, mirin, sugar and miso in a saucepan, mix well, then simmer over a low heat, stirring it carefully and constantly for 2–3 minutes. Once the mix has started to thicken and reduce, it is ready. Pour into a glass container to allow to cool. It can be stored for up to 3 weeks in an airtight container in the refrigerator, so, if you make some extra, it is a great sauce to have on hand for other dishes.

3. Once the tofu has been pressed, cut it into domino-shapes about 1.5cm/½ inch thick. Skewer one piece at a time (if using skewers), then bake for 30 minutes on the prepared tray. This dries out the tofu and intensifies its flavour. Leave the tofu on the baking tray.

4. With a teaspoon, spread the sauce evenly on one side of the tofu dominos to the edges. Grill (broil) for 3–4 minutes until the sauce begins to caramelize, sprinkle with the sesame seeds and serve immediately.

TWISTS

This *dengaku* dish is usually made with vegetables or tofu, with aubergine (eggplant) being the most popular. If you want to do this, simply use the same dressing on roasted aubergine to glaze, then grill for a further 5 minutes to let it caramelize. Occasionally white fish is used too, so if you want to make that variation it's best to use firmer fish, such as monkfish, hake or pollock.

KOREAN FRIED TOFU LETTUCE WRAPS

If you have tried Korean fried chicken, you will know that it is on a whole other level. This tofu twist on the iconic dish retains all the original's lip-smacking hallmarks – crispy, sharp, sweet and spicy – and you won't be able to stop at just one piece. Having experimented extensively to create the perfect crunch, a mix of plain flour and cornflour really nails it. Serve on crispy lettuce as a starter, or with rice.

Serves 4–6

For the tofu

100g/3½oz/¾ cup cornflour (corn starch)

100g/3½oz/¾ cup plain flour (all-purpose flour)

300g/10½oz firm tofu, drained for 20 minutes, pressed (see pages 14–15) and cut into 1cm/½ inch cubes

100ml/3½fl oz/scant ½ cup vegetable oil

For the sauce

3 tbsp tomato ketchup

2 tbsp gochujang

3 tbsp clear honey

3 tbsp brown sugar

2 tbsp rice vinegar, or Worcestershire sauce

1 tbsp light soy sauce

1 tsp finely chopped or grated garlic

1 tbsp toasted sesame oil

For the garnish

spring onions (scallions), finely sliced

1 tbsp toasted sesame seeds

6–8 lettuce leaves

1. In a mixing bowl, simply mix together all the ingredients for the sauce until you have a runny, blood-red liquid. Set aside.

2. Mix together both flours on a tray or large plate and use it to coat the tofu cubes evenly.

3. Heat the oil in a frying pan (skillet) until bubbling hot. With tongs or chopsticks, place the tofu pieces in the pan and cook for 3–4 minutes, turning, until lightly golden brown on all sides. It is important to use a pan that gives 1cm/½ inch of space around each tofu piece for maximum crispiness, so, if your pan is smaller, cook in batches. Rest the fried tofu on kitchen paper (paper towels) to soak up any excess oil.

4. Heat up a non-stick pan, pour the sauce in and wait for it to bubble and thicken. Quickly toss in the tofu; don't leave it in the pan too long or you will lose the crisp coating that you have worked so hard for.

5. Sprinkle with spring onions and toasted sesame seeds, then serve on lettuce leaves.

TWISTS

Mix up the textures by swapping some of the tofu for aubergine (eggplant) cubes. You can also top the dish with a variety of nuts or seeds instead of just using sesame – try crushed cashew nuts, peanuts or pine nuts for extra crunch.

THREE-CUP TOFU

This Chinese dish is named in the same way as pound cake; the clue is in the title! The three cups refer to the equal ratio of Chinese rice wine, toasted sesame oil and soy sauce… simple! Often cooked in a claypot and with chicken in place of tofu, this sauce is so versatile. I love it on seafood, too.

Serves 2

300g/10½oz firm tofu, drained and chopped into 1.5cm/½ inch cubes

70g 2½oz/½ cup cornflour (corn starch), plus 2 tsp

3 tbsp sunflower oil

1 medium red pepper (bell pepper), chopped into 1.5cm/½ inch cubes

2.5cm/1 inch piece fresh ginger, peeled and sliced into fine matchsticks

1 garlic clove, finely sliced

1 tbsp light soy sauce

1 tbsp dark soy sauce

2 tbsp toasted sesame oil

2 tbsp Shaoxing rice wine

1 tbsp caster sugar (superfine sugar)

1. Coat the tofu pieces evenly with the 70g/2½oz/½ cup cornflour.

2. Heat up a wide frying pan (skillet) or wok, add 2 tbsp of the sunflower oil and when hot add the tofu pieces slowly, turning them frequently until each side is crispy and golden. The tofu should sizzle when it hits the pan and you may have to cook it in several batches so as not to overcrowd the pan, which makes the tofu less crispy. Drain on kitchen paper (paper towels) while you get the rest of the ingredients ready.

3. Heat up a claypot or heavy-based saucepan over a medium heat. Warm up the remaining 1 tbsp sunflower oil for 1 minute before adding the red pepper, ginger and garlic. Stir-fry gently for another minute until the pepper starts to soften.

4. In a small bowl, mix together the soy sauces, sesame oil, rice wine and sugar until dissolved.

5. Add the sauce to the pan with the softened pepper and increase the heat to allow the sauce to bubble and thicken.

6. Once the sauce starts to reduce and the wine aroma has started to fill the room, mix the 2 tsp cornflour with 2 tbsp water in a small bowl and add it to the pan to thicken the sauce slightly. Add the tofu to the pan to coat with the sauce, but be careful not to leave it in the pan for too long or it will lose its crispiness.

TWISTS

Adding chicken thigh meat, chicken drumsticks or whole tiger prawns (jumbo shrimp) with their shells on, after the tofu has been added, makes a more authentic version of this classic dish.

CRISPY TOFU CHIPS WITH TERIYAKI DIP

This is a great way to enjoy the classic Japanese teriyaki sauce. Sweet and savoury, it is a moreish dip for piping-hot batons of crispy tofu. The sauce here makes a bigger batch than you need, which you can keep for other dishes too, such as grilled vegetables or noodles. I love keeping a small jar in the refrigerator for finishing off dishes. The key to super-crispy tofu here is to ensure you have squeezed out the excess moisture in the tofu, and for the oil to be sizzling hot.

Serves 2–3

For the tofu

300g/10½oz firm tofu, drained and pressed (see pages 14–15)

1 large egg

1 tsp light soy sauce

2 tbsp cornflour (corn starch)

2 tbsp plain flour (all-purpose flour)

2–3 tbsp olive oil

For the sauce

4 tbsp light soy sauce

4 tbsp sake

4 tbsp mirin

2 tbsp caster sugar (superfine sugar)

½ tsp minced fresh ginger

1. First make the sauce. Put all the liquid ingredients in a saucepan and cook until steaming hot, then add the sugar and ginger and stir to dissolve the sugar. Reduce the heat and continue to simmer for 15–20 minutes. Keep stirring and heating and tilting the pan slightly to check for bubbles starting to rise. Once this happens, the sauce is ready. For a thicker sauce, simmer for a further 10 minutes, although adding a little cornflour will help it thicken more quickly. This will keep in a sterilized jar (see page 25) for 2–3 weeks.

2. Slice the tofu into batons that make it easy to pick them up. If the tofu is still yielding some moisture, give it another 10-minute press once sliced, to remove any final liquid.

3. Crack the egg into a bowl and lightly beat, then add the soy sauce.

4. In another bowl, mix both flours together.

5. In a large flat frying pan (skillet), heat up the oil for 1 minute. Using chopsticks or tongs, lift each piece of tofu, dip it into the egg, then straight into the flour mix to coat all sides, then finally place the pieces into the hot oil.

6. Keep them turning in the pan so all the sides are nice and crispy. Once golden on all sides, transfer to sheets of kitchen paper (paper towels) to soak up the excess oil.

7. Serve with the teriyaki sauce, either as a dip or drizzled on top.

LIME & COCONUT CRISPY TOFU SALAD

This recipe really celebrates tropical flavours, with the coconut and zesty lime hurling tofu into the summer spotlight, ready for topping a colourful salad. If you love crunchy textures, this recipe is crunch squared. Serve with a bright salad full of snappy, fruity flavours such as mango and tomatoes. A light drizzle of miso mayonnaise completes the dish.

Serves 3–4

For the salad

4 tbsp light soy sauce

60g/2oz/¼ cup soft brown sugar

finely grated zest and juice of 1 lime

½ tbsp peeled and finely grated fresh ginger

400g/14oz firm tofu, drained for 20 minutes, pressed (see pages 14–15) and sliced into 1cm/½ inch cubes

2 tbsp plain flour (all-purpose flour)

2 tbsp cornflour (corn starch)

¼ tsp baking powder

3 tbsp cold water, plus extra if needed

120g/4½oz/1¼ cups panko crumbs

75g/2½oz/¾ cup unsweetened shredded coconut

4 tbsp vegetable oil, plus extra if needed

salad leaves, tomatoes, mango and red onion, to serve

For the miso mayonnaise

1 tbsp white miso paste

3 tbsp mayonnaise

2 tsp maple syrup

1 red chilli, deseeded and finely chopped

pinch of freshly ground black pepper

1. Warm the soy sauce and brown sugar in a small saucepan over a low heat until the sugar has dissolved, then add the lime zest and juice and the ginger.

2. Place the tofu pieces in a large box with a lid and pour the marinade over, then seal and refrigerate for 2 hours, flipping the tofu halfway through to ensure the flavours seep in all over. (I have often left it overnight and that works great, too.)

3. Combine the flour, cornflour, baking powder and water and whisk to combine, then refrigerate.

4. Pour the panko and shredded coconut onto a large tray and mix.

5. When you are ready to cook, remove the batter from the refrigerator and give it a stir. It should be a similar consistency as pancake batter. If it is too thick, add 1–2 tsp more water.

6. Line a tray with kitchen paper (paper towels) and set it next to the stove.

7. Heat the vegetable oil in a large non-stick frying pan (skillet) over a medium heat and, using tongs or chopsticks, dip the tofu into the batter, give it a quick shake, then dredge it through the panko-coconut mix, so the tofu is coated on all sides. Place it, piece by piece, in the pan. If the tofu doesn't sizzle straight away, the oil is not hot enough yet. Cook for 3 minutes on each side, until crispy and golden. If you cannot fit it all into one pan, then work in batches. Place each cooked piece on the kitchen paper-lined tray to absorb the excess oil.

8. If too much of the coating falls off into the oil, refresh it with new oil, to prevent burning.

9. As the tofu cools, prepare the miso mayonnaise by mixing the ingredients together in a bowl.

10. Serve the tofu with a colourful salad of chopped or sliced leaves, tomato, mango and red onion, drizzled with the miso mayonnaise.

SOFT & CHUNKY TOFU

Over the years, I've realized that I must have nursery tastebuds. I have always loved food that requires little effort to eat… just pass me a spoon. These meltingly tender chunky tofu dishes are the comforts of my childhood, and, what's more, they are super-quick to put together, as there is hardly any prep required for the tofu itself.

For these recipes, you want to choose a slightly porous and bouncy tofu that can carry flavours well. Tofu that is marked as 'medium-firm' or 'soft' is fine, just drain it for at least 20 minutes in a sieve; there is usually no need to press it, though you will for some of the recipes in this chapter. Avoid buying silken tofu, as it is a little too fragile for these dishes.

These dishes all partner up deliciously with something carby, as it would be a crime not to mop these silky sauces up with steamed rice or noodles.

MA PO TOFU WITH BUTTON MUSHROOMS

This is one for the spice lovers. The peppery heat hits you right between the eyes, with only a moment of relief offered by the calming tofu before you dive in for more. The dish hails from the spice province of Sichuan and the name means 'pock-marked old woman's tofu', after the legendary lady who originally sold the dish. Despite its punchy heat, this is actually a delicate recipe that celebrates tofu's wobbly pannacotta-like texture, akin to perfect poached eggs. The button mushrooms bring a gentle bite to the dish. Serve with fluffy steamed rice, and a towel for mopping your forehead.

Serves 4

4 tbsp vegetable oil

4 spring onions (scallions), green parts only, finely chopped

4 tbsp Sichuan chilli bean paste

2 tbsp finely chopped or grated garlic

2 tbsp peeled and finely chopped or grated fresh ginger

½ tsp freshly ground white pepper

100ml/3½fl oz/scant ½ cup water

600g/1lb 5oz firm or soft tofu, drained for 20 minutes and cut into 2.5cm/1 inch cubes

10 small button mushrooms, kept whole

2 tsp potato flour or corn flour

To serve (all optional)

coriander (cilantro)

2 pinches crushed Sichuan peppercorns

steamed rice and greens

1. Heat the oil in a frying pan (skillet), then throw in the spring onions, chilli bean paste and garlic. Cook for 2–3 minutes to allow the flavours to infuse. Stir in the ginger, white pepper and water.

2. Place the tofu carefully into the pan and stir the sauce around it, then reduce the heat and add the mushrooms.

3. In a small bowl, mix the potato flour with 1 tbsp water until smooth, then pour this mixture into the pan while stirring gently, to thicken the sauce around the tofu and mushrooms.

4. Serve immediately scattered with coriander and Sichuan pepper, if you like, with steamed rice and greens.

TWISTS

Traditionally, minced (ground) pork is added to this dish, so if you would like to try that, add 100g/3½oz/scant ½ cup minced pork at the same time as the ginger and cook it through before adding the tofu. Chopped prawns (shrimp) can also add an element of texture and sweetness instead of the mushrooms, if you prefer.

POACHED TOFU WITH 'STRANGE FLAVOUR' SESAME DRESSING

This sauce is inspired by a poached chicken dish in Sichuanese cuisine, oddly named 'strange flavoured chicken'. Don't worry, there's nothing strange about it, it's just an unusual translation! 'Strange flavour' is one of the '26 flavours' in Sichuanese cooking – others include 'fish flavour' and 'numbing and hot flavour' – and this is definitely one of my favourites.

This sauce – creamy, nutty, salty, with just a hint of Sichuan pepper – is great on vegetables and leaner meats such as turkey or chicken. It works fantastically with tofu, of course, contrasting against its sweet, calm flavours. This is a great quick dish, ready in 10 minutes! If you can't find Sichuan peppercorns, though I highly recommend you try to seek them out, regular black pepper will also work.

Serves 2–4

3 tbsp tahini

2 tbsp toasted sesame oil

1½ tbsp caster sugar (superfine sugar)

1½ tsp Chinkiang vinegar

1 tbsp light soy sauce

½ tsp ground Sichuan peppercorns

½ tsp sea salt flakes

200g/7oz firm tofu, drained for 20 minutes and sliced into long matchstick strips

toasted sesame seeds and coriander (cilantro) sprigs, to serve

1. In a bowl, mix together all the ingredients except the tofu.

2. Bring a large saucepan of water to the boil and simmer the tofu strips for 2 minutes until warmed through. Drain on kitchen paper (paper towels), being careful not to break up the tofu.

3. To present the dish, lay the tofu strips all facing in the same direction, then drizzle the sauce on top. Scatter with the toasted sesame seeds and coriander and serve.

SMOKED TOFU OKONOMIYAKI

Okonomiyaki is a kind of Japanese pancake, or even pizza… but neither of these terms really does justice to the knock-out flavours of this street-food classic. I have fond memories of eating this with beloved friends, accompanied with jugs of beer and sprawling plates of edamame beans. Fantastic as a vegetarian dish (though traditionally made with seafood, bacon and vegetables) the smoked tofu here adds lovely dark flavours whether you are cooking it in a frying pan (skillet) or on a proper teppanyaki plate. My recipe is based on Osakan-style okonomiyaki (made from shredded cabbage) rather than Hiroshima-style (made from noodles), because I love the density of these veggie-packed pancakes. After you have made this once, you can start to get really creative with the toppings: it pairs well with seafood, mackerel, bacon, cheese… *okonomiyaki* literally means 'however you like it', so permission is ready-granted! If you don't have Japanese mayonnaise, just stir 2 teaspoons of caster sugar into the same amount of regular mayonnaise.

Serves 4

For the okonomiyaki

250g/9oz/2 cups plain flour (all-purpose flour)

2 tsp baking powder

300ml/10fl oz/1¼ cups water

4 large eggs

500g/1lb 2oz/5 cups shredded white cabbage

6 spring onions (scallions), finely chopped

100g/3½oz/generous ½ cup sweetcorn (corn)

vegetable oil, for frying

200g/7oz smoked tofu, sliced into batons

To serve

150ml/5fl oz/⅔ cup Japanese mayonnaise (or see recipe introduction)

250ml/9fl oz/generous 1 cup Tonkatsu sauce (see page 42)

finely ground nori

1. Sift the flour and baking powder together in a large bowl. Gradually pour in the water, mixing until smooth. Crack in the eggs and whisk until fully combined.

2. In another large bowl, mix together the cabbage, spring onions and sweetcorn.

3. Pour the wet mixture into the dry bowl and fold together. The cabbage will start to lose its volume and become heavy with the batter.

4. Heat a heavy-based frying pan (skillet) over a high heat and drizzle evenly with oil.

5. Using a large serving spoon or ladle, scoop up a portion of batter and carefully place it into the pan, leaving at least 5cm/2 inches of space between each pancake and fitting 2–3 into the pan. Place pieces of the smoked tofu in their centres.

6. Reduce the heat and cook for 2 minutes, until you see the edges of the pancakes start to crisp up and turn golden. Carefully flip the pancakes (I find using 2 spatulas helpful!) and cook for a further 5 minutes, until cooked through.

7. Flip the pancakes one more time and cook for a final minute.

8. To finish, create a criss-cross pattern using the mayonnaise and tonkatsu sauce, then sprinkle with nori. Serve immediately.

OKINAWAN TOFU WITH BITTER MELON

This dish famously hails from the sunny island of Okinawa. Some of you may know it as the Japanese island where the greatest number of centenarians live, while others may know it as the place where Karate Kid's Mr Miyagi comes from! There are clearly many reasons why this island is important, but for me, it is all about this dish. *Goya chanpuru* is a stir-fried dish traditionally made with pork belly, tofu, bitter melon and fried egg. It is a real journey of a recipe, full of flavour and contrast: sweetness and richness from the pork, creaminess from the tofu, a sharp palate cleanser from the bitter melon, then a golden lingering from the egg. Bitter melon can be divisive, so, if you are unsure, swap in marrow or courgette (zucchini) for a milder experience. *Chanpuru* refers to Okinawan stir-fried dishes of any mix of ingredients, often including tofu and other vegetables such as beansprouts, so feel free to freestyle once you have nailed this classic.

Serves 2

1 small bitter melon

1 tsp fine sea salt, plus extra to season

350g/12oz medium-firm tofu, drained

3 tbsp vegetable oil

2 pinches of freshly ground white pepper, plus extra to season

1 tsp light soy sauce

60ml/2¼fl oz/4 tbsp dashi (see pages 27–8)

1 large egg with a deep yellow yolk

1. First prepare the bitter melon: slice it in half lengthways, scrape out the seeds, then slice each half into 1cm/½ inch thick half moons. Place in a colander.

2. Sprinkle with the sea salt and leave for 10 minutes for some of the bitter juices to leach out. Then rinse off the excess salt.

3. Take the tofu and, using your hands, tear into bite-sized pieces, each about 2cm/¾ inch thick. It doesn't need to be neat.

4. In a large frying pan (skillet), heat up 2 tbsp of the oil and gently fry the tofu pieces until lightly browned all over. Lift them carefully out of the pan and on to kitchen paper (paper towels) to absorb any excess oil.

5. Add the remaining 1 tbsp of oil to the same pan and fry the bitter melon until cooked through and soft, about 4–5 minutes. Return the tofu to

the pan, then add the white pepper, soy sauce and dashi.

6. Lightly beat the egg in a small bowl and season with a pinch of salt and white pepper. Add it to the pan so it surrounds the tofu and bitter melon.

7. Do not move the egg around.

8. As soon as the egg is cooked and golden, serve immediately with steamed rice.

TWIST

For the complete experience, add thin slices of pork belly or bacon to the pan just before the melon goes in, so the richness of the meat is taken on by the vegetables. You will need about 6 slices, or 150g/5½oz for this dish. Spam is a surprisingly popular addition to this dish, reflecting the US Navy's influence in Okinawa.

INDO-CHINESE CHILLI TOFU

I first tried this in a simple roadside cafe in Mumbai, served with a heap of chapatis, and I just couldn't get enough. The purist in me was highly sceptical of Indo-Chinese fusion dishes – despite my host's enthusiasm for them – but this recipe seriously won me over. In fact, I spent the rest of my trip trying out as many Indo-Chinese foods as I could, which combine fiery Indian spices with Chinese sweet soy and glossy sauces: a match made in culinary heaven.

Serves 2 as a main course, or 4 as part of a larger meal

600g/1lb 5oz firm tofu, drained and pressed (see pages 14–15), then cut into 2.5cm/1 inch cubes

100g/3½oz/¾ cup cornflour (corn starch), plus 1 tsp

3 tbsp vegetable oil

2 tsp cumin seeds

2 tsp minced fresh ginger

2 tsp minced garlic

1 onion, cut into 2.5cm/1 inch cubes

1 tbsp ground coriander

3 tsp caster sugar (superfine sugar)

¼ tsp fine sea salt

1 tsp ground black pepper

2 small finger chillies, finely chopped

1 green pepper (bell pepper), cut into 2.5cm/1 inch cubes

2 tbsp light soy sauce

2 tbsp tomato purée (tomato paste)

1 tbsp fresh coriander (cilantro), finely chopped

1. Coat the tofu with the 100g/3½oz/¾ cup cornflour so that it is covered on all sides.

2. Heat 2 tbsp of the oil in a non-stick or cast-iron pan. Sauté the tofu cubes on all sides until they are golden brown, then remove and drain on kitchen paper (paper towels).

3. Heat the remaining 1 tbsp oil and add the cumin seeds. When they start to spit, add the ginger, and then the garlic and onion.

4. Sauté for 3–4 minutes until the onion becomes transparent, then add the ground coriander, sugar, salt, black pepper and chillies.

5. Toss to coat with the spices, then add the green pepper. Stir-fry until the pepper starts to soften but still has a good bite to it. Now return the tofu to the pan.

6. In a small bowl, mix together the soy sauce, the 1 tsp cornflour mixed with 100ml/3½fl oz/scant ½ cup water, and the tomato purée.

7. Slowly pour this into the pan and heat up. The sauce will slowly thicken until it is glossy.

8. Sprinkle with the fresh coriander and serve hot with rice.

KUNG PAO TOFU WITH MACADAMIA NUTS

This sweet-spicy-sour sauce is just the ticket to wake up your tastebuds, with the rich buttery nuts complementing the dense and creamy tofu. I really recommend seeking out Sichuan peppercorns, to enjoy the tongue-tingling effects of this special spice. You may have tried a chicken version of this dish in a Chinese restaurant before; this version is less sweet and more refreshing, with crunchy celery bursting in to add another layer of fragrant flavour. This recipe comes together very quickly, so it's best to have everything chopped and ready to go before you start cooking.

Serves 2 as a main course, or 4 as part of a larger meal

For the tofu

3 tbsp sunflower oil

7 dried chillies

1 tsp whole Sichuan peppercorns

300g/10½oz firm tofu, drained and cut into 1.5cm/½ inch cubes

3 garlic cloves, roughly chopped

1 small thumb of fresh ginger, minced

3 spring onions (scallions), chopped into 1.5cm/½ inch pieces

75g/2¾oz/½ cup macadamia nuts, lightly toasted

2 celery sticks, cut into dice of a similar size to the nuts

For the sauce

2 tbsp caster sugar (superfine sugar)

1 tsp potato flour

2 tsp dark soy sauce

4 tsp light soy sauce

2 tbsp Chinkiang vinegar

2 tsp tomato purée (tomato paste)

2 tsp toasted sesame oil

4 tbsp water

1. In a small bowl, mix together all the sauce ingredients. Set aside.

2. Heat up a wok or frying pan (skillet) and add the oil, warming it up for a few minutes until bubbles begin to appear.

3. Add the dried chillies and Sichuan peppercorns and stir-fry for 3–4 minutes to release the flavours.

4. Add the tofu pieces and stir-fry to coat them with the spicy oil.

5. Add the garlic and ginger and allow to sizzle for 2 minutes before adding the spring onions.

6. Once the onions have softened, add the sauce ingredients to the pan and slowly simmer, as the sauce thickens.

7. Finally add the nuts and celery to the pan, mix together with the rest of the ingredients and serve immediately. Don't let the nuts or celery soften too much in the hot sauce, or you'll lose their contrasting crunchy texture.

TWISTS

The macadamia nuts could be swapped out for cashews, peanuts or hazelnuts instead, or you can add small cubes of chicken thigh meat to make a more traditional version of the dish.

BAKED MAPLE-MISO TOFU RICE BOWL

I don't oven-cook tofu that often, usually preferring the instant flash of heat from a pan, but recently I discovered the joy of baking. Firstly, you can go off and prepare other dishes while the oven is doing the hard work, and secondly you end up using a lot less oil than you do when frying, but with this recipe you still get those sweet golden flavours. Baking also makes the tofu firmer, so it's great for adding texture to your meal.

Glazed with an umami-rich and sweet sauce, this tofu rice bowl is a quick weeknight meal that will be ready by the time the rice is cooked. Serve with greens such as pak choi or broccoli and storecupboard staples such as sweetcorn, eggs and pickles. Add extra crunch with nuts and seeds, too.

Serves 2

For the rice bowl

180g/6oz/1 scant cup jasmine or Japanese rice

3 tbsp white miso paste

2 tbsp toasted sesame oil

1 tbsp maple syrup

300g/10½oz firm tofu, drained for 20 minutes and pressed (see pages 14–15), then sliced into 1cm/½ inch slabs

1 garlic clove, finely chopped

1 tbsp olive oil

2 heads of pak choi (bok choy), quartered lengthways

toasted sesame seeds

For the spicy miso mayonnaise

4 tbsp mayonnaise

1 tbsp red miso paste

1 tbsp chilli sauce

1 tsp caster sugar (superfine sugar)

For the other toppings (all optional)

olive oil

2 eggs, soft-boiled and halved

2 tbsp finely chopped chives

1 small cucumber, finely chopped

radishes

edamame beans

Japanese pickles

cashew nuts

1. Cook the rice according to the packet instructions (package directions).

2. Meanwhile, in a small bowl, mix together the white miso paste, sesame oil and maple syrup, then pour this into a shallow tray. Lay the tofu pieces in the sauce and turn over to cover on both sides.

3. Line a baking tray with foil and preheat the oven to 200°C fan/ 220°C/425°F/gas mark 7. Place each piece of tofu carefully in a row on the prepared tray and bake for 5 minutes, or until golden. Flip and bake on the other side for the same cooking time.

4. Meanwhile, mix together all the ingredients for the spicy miso mayonnaise in a small bowl.

5. In a frying pan (skillet), sauté the garlic in the oil for a few minutes, before adding the pak choi. Stir-fry for a few minutes, then divide the rice, tofu and greens between two bowls. Sprinkle with toasted sesame seeds then drizzle with the spicy miso mayo.

6. Add whichever extra toppings you like, then serve.

CURRIED CORONATION TOFU

I love a creamy sandwich filling: Marie Rose sauce with prawns (shrimp); cheese and coleslaw; egg and cress… and this one, unashamedly based on the classic Coronation chicken. Firm tofu pieces are coddled in a thick sauce, surrounded by raisins, mango and sweet curry flavours; it is a delightful new arrival in my life. Great in sandwiches, or to top salads and baked potatoes.

Fills 6 sandwiches very generously

150ml/5fl oz/⅔ cup mayonnaise

150ml/5fl oz/⅔ cup Greek yogurt

2 tsp Worcestershire sauce

2 tbsp medium curry powder

3 tbsp mango chutney

70g/2½oz/½ cup dried apricots, finely chopped

40g/1½oz/¼ cup golden raisins, the bigger the better

1 thumb of fresh ginger, peeled and grated

300g/10½oz block of firm tofu, drained for 20 minutes and chopped into 1cm/½ inch cubes

handful of coriander (cilantro), chopped

½ tsp sea salt flakes

pinch of freshly ground black pepper

1. In a large mixing bowl, simply mix together the mayonnaise and yogurt until combined. Add the Worcestershire sauce, curry powder and mango chutney and mix thoroughly. Add the dried fruits and the grated ginger and mix again.

2. Carefully fold in the tofu, being careful not to mix too hard, which would break up the pieces.

3. Add the coriander and season with the salt and pepper.

TWISTS

Adding some finely chopped walnuts or celery brings extra crunch and texture.

To make this recipe vegan, simply swap the mayonnaise with vegan mayonnaise and the Greek yogurt with soya or almond milk yogurt.

SPINACH & CORIANDER MASALA TOFU

This chilli chutney is sublime. I always make extra to perk up a veggie soup or add more heat to a curry. Slathered on tofu and griddled, it is inspired by an amazing paneer dish I enjoyed in Delhi. The spices linger, but it's gentle and warming rather than chilli-hot. Giving tofu the Indian treatment is a no-brainer, as it holds up well against bold, contrasting flavours. This dish is an easy, prep-ahead meal for the next day, and, if skewered, can also bring a spicy twist to a barbecue. Choose a firm tofu so that it does not crumble when skewered or stir-fried.

Serves 4 as a stir-fry/Makes 6 large skewers

For the tofu

500g/1lb 5oz firm tofu, drained for 20 minutes and pressed (see pages 14–15)

2 small onions, cut into wedges

1 red pepper (bell pepper), if making skewers

200g/7oz/7 cups fresh spinach, if making a griddled or fried dish

For the marinade

2 small green chillies, seeds left in

6 garlic cloves, finely chopped or grated

2 handfuls of fresh coriander (cilantro), finely chopped, plus extra to serve

2 tsp ground coriander

2 tsp garam masala

2 tsp sea salt flakes

1 tsp ground turmeric

2 tbsp Greek yogurt

100ml/3½fl oz/scant ½ cup vegetable oil, plus extra (optional) for cooking

1. Finely chop or blend the chillies, garlic and chopped coriander to create a paste, then mix with all the other marinade ingredients in a box or bowl with a lid.

2. Cut the tofu into equal-sized cubes and the red pepper (if using) and onion into pieces of a similar size. Gently stir them into the marinade and leave overnight, or for at least 8 hours, to let the flavours really do their work.

3. If you are cooking on a griddle pan (grill pan) or in a frying pan (skillet), simply heat up the pan with a little drizzle of oil and sear the tofu and onion on all sides, using kitchen tongs to turn the pieces individually. Add the spinach to the pan 2 minutes before serving. If you are cooking on a barbecue, skewer the tofu pieces with the red pepper and onion alternately and cook them for 3–4 minutes on each side.

4. Scatter with more coriander before serving, and enjoy with fresh salad.

BEAR'S PAW TOFU

One of my favourite food memoirs (by one of my food heroes, too) is Fuchsia Dunlop's *Shark's Fin & Sichuan Pepper*. In it she shares how she found out about the morbid practice of capturing bears in east Asia for ancient exotic dishes, despite laws that seek to protect them. I was therefore moved to find that vegetarian dishes have been invented to mimic the original recipes without the cruelty. Bear's paw tofu is very similar to the 'countryside tofu' dish that is well known in Sichuan. The tofu is pan-fried rather than deep-fried, with only a small amount of oil, to create a pattern on the tofu that is apparently similar to that of a cooked bear's paw (so they say; I'm glad to admit I wouldn't know), before sauces and other vegetables are added. This is a quick ten-minute recipe, perfect for quick dinners, and deeply satisfying.

Serves 4

500g/1lb 2oz firm tofu

vegetable oil, for deep-frying

2 tbsp Sichuan chilli bean paste

4 garlic cloves, sliced finely

1 thumb of fresh ginger, peeled and sliced into fine coins

1 tsp Sichuan peppercorns, ground

300ml/10½fl oz/1¼ cups dashi (see pages 27–8), or chicken stock

½ tsp brown sugar

1 tsp light soy sauce

4 spring onions (scallions), finely sliced into rings

½ tsp cornflour (corn starch)

1. Drain and press the tofu for 20 minutes (see pages 14–15), then slice into rectangular pieces around 1.5cm/½ inch thick.

2. Heat a large saucepan with vegetable oil about 5cm/2 inches deep; it should reach no more than one-third of the way up the sides of the pan. As always when deep-frying, be very careful and do not leave the kitchen or take a telephone call.

3. Fry the tofu in batches of 2–3 pieces only (don't overcrowd the pan) and flip them so that they become lightly golden on both sides. Drain on kitchen paper (paper towels) to absorb any excess oil.

4. Remove the oil from the pan. Return it to a high heat and fry the chilli bean paste for a few seconds before adding the garlic, ginger and Sichuan pepper. Stir-fry for a further 30 seconds.

5. In a small bowl, whisk the dashi or chicken stock, sugar and soy sauce. Pour it into the pan and let it bubble for 1 minute before carefully adding the tofu pieces.

6. Bring the mixture to the boil, then reduce the heat and simmer for a further 4 minutes.

7. Add half the spring onions and reduce the heat once more.

8. Mix the cornflour in a small bowl with 1 tsp water, then add to the pan evenly, so the sauce thickens slowly.

9. As soon as the sauce begins to thicken, serve up the tofu sprinkled with the remaining spring onions. Serve with rice.

TWISTS

Shiitake, straw or button mushrooms can give texture to the dish.

ROASTED PEANUT TOFU CURRY

I am not peanut butter-mad, but I do love peanut curries. Smooth and silky, the spices here are tempered by the gentle creamy nuttiness to create a happy home for tofu. This curry recipe is one that I cook often as a base for sweet potato, aubergine (eggplant), tofu or fish. It is an easy dish that should be part of your repertoire, too. It's the curry pictured on the left-hand side of page 73.

Serves 4

150g/5½oz/1¼ cups red-skinned peanuts

1 small onion, diced

150ml/5fl oz/⅔ cup vegetable or sunflower oil, plus 2 tbsp

4 garlic cloves, finely chopped

1 thumb of fresh ginger, peeled and minced

25g/1oz/2 tbsp soft brown sugar

1 tbsp ground coriander

1 tbsp ground cumin

1½ tsp cumin seeds

2 tsp chilli powder

1 large tomato, roughly chopped

2 handfuls of fresh coriander (cilantro), finely chopped, plus extra to serve

500g/1lb 2oz firm tofu, drained for 20 minutes (see page 14)

100ml/3½fl oz/scant ½ cup water, plus extra if needed

rice or naan bread, to serve

1. Toast the peanuts in a dry frying pan (skillet) for 3–4 minutes, then blend into a fine powder. Tip into a large bowl.

2. In the same pan, fry the onion in 1 tbsp of oil over a medium heat, until lightly browned and soft, adding the garlic for the last minute of cooking.

3. Mix the sugar, spices and tomato into the bowl with the peanuts, add the browned onion and garlic, then pour over the 150ml/5fl oz/⅔ cup oil, stirring to make a curry sauce. Finally, mix in the chopped coriander.

4. Chop the drained tofu into chunks. Heat the remaining 1 tbsp of oil in a large frying pan (skillet) and fry the tofu, turning, until golden brown on all sides.

5. Slowly heat the curry sauce in a saucepan, adding the water.

6. Add the tofu to the curry sauce and simmer for a further 10 minutes. Check the consistency and add a splash or so more water, if you prefer a looser curry. Serve with a final scattering of coriander and a generous helping of rice or naan bread.

THAI COCONUT CURRY

This curry base is fantastic for all Thai green curries. The bold flavours are unapologetic and, together with lightly pan-fried tofu, make a flavoursome but light dinner. I love having a stash of this sauce in the freezer, ready for a last-minute weekday dinner. Add vegetables and serve with rice, or thin it down with stock and add rice noodles for a hearty noodle soup. Jackfruit, prawns (shrimp), crab or chicken are also great in this curry.

Serves 4

For the curry paste

4 lemon grass stalks, tough outer leaves discarded

6 tbsp fresh coriander (cilantro), chopped

4 garlic cloves, chopped

5–6 small green chillies, to taste, deseeded and chopped

2.5cm/1 inch piece of galangal, peeled and chopped

2.5cm/1 inch piece of fresh ginger, peeled and chopped

2 shallots, peeled and chopped

1 tsp ground cumin

1 tsp ground coriander

1 tsp finely grated lime zest

For the curry

500g/1lb 2oz medium-soft tofu

vegetable oil, for frying

200g/7oz/1½ cups sweet potatoes, peeled and chopped into cubes

1 red onion, finely chopped

400ml/14fl oz/1¾ cups coconut milk

400ml/14fl oz/1¾ cups vegetable stock

10 lime leaves

1 tbsp fish sauce, or red miso paste

½ tsp freshly ground black pepper

20g/¾oz/1 packed cup basil leaves, torn

20g/¾oz/1 packed cup fresh coriander (cilantro) leaves and stalks, roughly chopped

1. First make the curry paste. Slice the lemon grass finely and blitz in a food processor with all the other curry paste ingredients until you have a thick paste. Transfer to a glass jar to prevent staining.

2. Cut the tofu into bite-sized pieces and, in a hot frying pan (skillet), fry with a little vegetable oil until slightly golden on all sides. Set aside.

3. In a saucepan, boil the sweet potatoes for 5–6 minutes until tender, then drain and set aside.

4. In a large casserole, fry the red onion in a little more vegetable oil until soft and tender, then add the coconut milk and stock and bring to a simmer.

5. Next add the lime leaves and par-boiled sweet potatoes and simmer for 2 minutes before adding 4 large tbsp of the curry paste, the fish sauce or miso, black pepper, and half the basil and coriander. Reduce the heat and simmer for 10 minutes, stirring occasionally.

6. Add the tofu and a further 1 tbsp curry paste and simmer for another 5 minutes.

7. Stir in the last of the basil and coriander and serve.

TWISTS

Swapping the vegetable stock for chicken stock adds deeper flavour. This curry base is great with chicken and seafood curries as well as vegetables with an absorbent texture, such as potatoes, courgettes (zucchini), aubergines (eggplant) and mushrooms.

EGG & CHIVE TOFU

The golden aroma of fried egg is hard to resist. Across Asia, egg dishes are often whipped, lightly seasoned, then flash-fried to bring out that yolky richness before being served straight away. This quick eggy coating for tofu makes it a super-quick and nutritious dinner. For me, this is a speedy, reliable topping for ramen noodles and rice bowls: you can enjoy a meal in minutes.

Serves 2

300g/10½oz firm tofu, drained and pressed (see pages 14–15)

2 eggs

1 tsp soy sauce

pinch of freshly ground white pepper

2 tbsp finely chopped chives, plus extra to serve

1 tsp toasted sesame oil

2 tbsp sunflower or vegetable oil

1. Slice the tofu into slabs 1cm/½ inch thick and in domino-shaped pieces.

2. In a large bowl, lightly beat the eggs and season with the soy sauce and white pepper before adding the chives.

3. Put the pieces of tofu into the bowl of egg mixture – the egg and chives will cling to them.

4. In a wide, flat frying pan (skillet), heat both types of oil, then, using tongs or chopsticks, lift the tofu piece-by-piece into the pan; the egg will begin to cook immediately. As soon as each piece turns golden, flip it over. Keep adding more pieces of tofu to the pan until it is filled without any overlap, pouring any remaining egg mixture on top.

5. Once each piece of tofu has been flipped once, cook for a further minute before lifting out of the pan to serve. Take care not to overcook it, or the egg will be a little rubbery: you want a fluffy coating here.

6. Sprinkle with extra chopped chives and serve.

MASHED TOFU

I don't know why I avoided mashing tofu for so long. Perhaps the purist in me had an issue with smashing those delicate bricks… But, once I'd got over it, a whole new world of tofu beckoned, as mashed tofu entwines and dances with other ingredients. Now, I even find the act of mashing tofu pleasurable!

Most mashed dishes suit a variety of tofu with less moisture, as any excess water will bleed out once you have served a recipe up: not a good look. So choose a firm tofu, drained for at least 20 minutes; pressing can help you get the last drops of moisture out.

This is fast and furious tofu, so don't be shy; pulverize it with gusto and let those flavours mingle. These dishes are both satisfying to make and comforting to eat.

CHILLI BUTTER TURMERIC TOFU SCRAMBLE

I want to put a massive red asterisk on this recipe and say that this is *the best* scrambled tofu I have ever eaten. We probably cook it once a fortnight in our house. I admit that I was once a scrambled tofu sceptic: I love eggs and refused to believe that anything else could come close, so why bother? But this tofu scramble is something else. Once you have tried it, you will believe the hype. This is effectively a mashed tofu stir-fry that is brought to life with a custard-like cheesy, spicy sauce that comes together very quickly and delightfully. The tofu takes on the flavours impressively, while staying delicate and wobbly like just-set custard. The keys to this dish are fresh moist tofu and nutritional yeast, which is really worth scouting out from health food stores. Don't be a fool like I was; embrace the tofu scramble!

Serves 2–3

3 tbsp olive oil

1 large red onion, finely sliced

½ red pepper (bell pepper), cut into long strips

2 garlic cloves, finely chopped or grated

2 tbsp unsalted butter

1 tsp Dijon mustard

300g/10½oz firm tofu, drained for 20 minutes

1 tbsp nutritional yeast flakes

1½ tsp ground turmeric

1½ tsp smoked paprika

35g/1¼oz/¼ cup plain flour (all-purpose flour)

1 tsp sea salt flakes

250ml/9fl oz/1 cup soya/oat milk, or regular milk

1–2 tsp chilli flakes

2 handfuls of baby spinach

handful of chopped coriander (cilantro)

1 tbsp chopped jalapeños, to serve (optional)

toasted pitta (pita) bread or sourdough bread, to serve

1. Heat the oil in a large saucepan and fry the onion, red pepper and garlic for 3–4 minutes until softened, then add the butter and mustard and stir together.

2. Crumble the tofu in gently, allowing some pieces to stay chunky.

3. In a small bowl, mix together the yeast, turmeric, paprika, flour and salt.

4. In a small saucepan, warm up the soya milk until bubbling, then stir it into the bowl of dry ingredients.

It will start to thicken up quickly, so make sure you keep beating it until smooth, using a wooden spoon.

5. Pour the sauce over the tofu, a little at a time, stirring it gently in and making sure the flavours are well mixed together. Add the chilli flakes and baby spinach and stir again, just to wilt the spinach leaves.

6. Turn off the heat and stir in the chopped coriander and jalapeños, if using, before serving with toasted pitta or sourdough bread.

TOFU SHIRAE SALAD

With all the sweet creaminess of potato salad, but also the satisfying crunch of coleslaw, this dish belongs in the Japanese food hall of fame. It is cooling, calming and light, a perfect match for strong flavours such as grilled fish or meat. The black olives are not traditional here, but I love their sweet, deep tang. Traditionally, edamame beans and hijiki seaweed are added, but I find the olives bring lots of flavour and I always have them in. This is easy to make for picnics, packed lunches and to serve alongside barbecues. The key is to patiently drain the tofu so it soaks up the flavours really well, while avoiding a runny sauce. You find this dish everywhere in Japan, from the tops of Buddhist temples down to the *combini* convenience stores; a dish for everyone.

Serves 2 as a main course, or 4 as a side dish

100g/3½oz/scant ¾ cup fine green beans (string beans)

3–4 dried shiitake or porcini mushrooms, soaked in hot water for 1–2 hours until fully hydrated, then drained and sliced

3 tbsp toasted sesame seeds, plus 1 tbsp extra to serve

1 tbsp tahini

1 tsp mirin (optional)

2 tsp white miso paste

1 tsp sea salt flakes

1½ tbsp caster sugar (superfine sugar)

120g/4¼oz firm tofu, drained for 20 minutes and pressed (see pages 14–15)

50g/1¾oz/1 cup carrots, julienned

50g/1¾oz/¼ cup pitted black olives, halved

1. Simmer the green beans in boiling water for 3–4 minutes until al dente, then lift out with a slotted spoon, cool and dry on kitchen paper (paper towels). Don't cook them for too long, as you want this salad to have a bit of crunch. Add the sliced shiitake mushrooms to the boiling water and simmer for 5 minutes, then drain.

2. In a pestle and mortar or a spice grinder, crush the toasted sesame seeds to a powder. In a mixing bowl, combine the crushed seeds with the tahini, mirin (if using), miso, salt and sugar and mix until fully combined.

3. Mash the tofu until completely broken, then add it to the sesame and miso mix.

4. Finally fold the carrots, beans, mushrooms and olives through the sauce and top with sesame seeds.

TWISTS

This dressing is fantastic with lots of vegetables, especially woodier ones such as tenderstem broccoli (broccolini) and asparagus. Prawns (shrimp), chopped egg and oyster mushrooms also add interesting new textures and work well with these creamy, nutty flavours. It's also great eaten on its own as a dip.

LEMON MISO TOFU STUFFED PEPPERS

This dish is inspired by a beloved Chinese dish called 'stuffed treasures', where fluffy prawn (shrimp) paste is nudged into the uneven interior of peppers (bell peppers), fried, then drizzled with a rich sauce. This lighter version brings together my two favourite ingredients – tofu and miso – and lifts them to zesty heights. This dish is bright and flavourful and very simple to make. The stuffed peppers can be kept warm in the oven until they are ready to be sauced. Serve with salad or noodles, or as a starter.

Serves 4

1 red pepper (bell pepper)

1 green pepper (bell pepper)

1 yellow pepper (bell pepper)

2 tbsp olive oil

250g/9oz firm tofu, drained for 20 minutes and pressed (see pages 14–15)

1 egg yolk

2–3 tsp cornflour (corn starch), plus extra for dusting

½ tsp sea salt flakes

2 tbsp chopped chives, plus extra to serve

4 tbsp panko crumbs

For the lemon miso sauce

6 tbsp white miso paste

6 tbsp mirin

60g/2¼oz/generous ¼ cup golden caster sugar (superfine sugar), unrefined if possible

finely grated zest and juice of 1 lemon

1. Preheat the oven to 180°C fan/ 200°C/400°F/gas mark 6.

2. Halve the peppers, then halve the pieces again to create segments for filling. Drizzle with the olive oil and roast for 10 minutes.

3. Now make the miso tofu mix. The key is to really drain the tofu well, as any water will make the filling too wet. Break up the tofu with your hands into a large bowl. Add the egg yolk, cornflour and salt and mix well.

4. In a small bowl, mix together all the ingredients for the lemon miso sauce. Pour 100ml/3½fl oz/scant ½ cup of it into the tofu mix and stir well. Finally, add the chives.

5. Take the peppers out of the oven and dust them with cornflour, before carefully filling them with the tofu mix with a spoon, taking care to smooth it into all the spaces, then levelling each stuffed pepper using the back of the spoon. The tofu should be compactly pushed in and level on the top.

6. Sprinkle the panko evenly over the stuffed peppers, return them to the oven and bake for a further 20–25 minutes until golden.

7. When ready to serve, drizzle with the remaining miso lemon sauce and scatter with chopped chives.

DOUBLE-COOKED SPICY TOFU BURGERS

I love sinking my teeth into a deeply filled burger, but usually pass on veggie burgers, finding them lacking in flavour and texture. Due to this prejudice, it has taken me some time to perfect this patty. Key to its design is the double cooking: frying gives a great crispy texture, while baking helps to firm it up for extra bite. This is a tofu burger that doesn't compromise on texture or flavour and any leftovers are also great cold the next day, with a little relish.

Makes 4

For the burgers

350g/12oz fresh pressed tofu, or firm tofu that has been drained and pressed (see pages 14–15)

2 tbsp sun-dried tomatoes, puréed

2 tbsp sriracha

handful of mint leaves, finely chopped

handful of basil leaves, finely chopped

handful of coriander (cilantro), finely chopped

1 small shallot, finely chopped

finely grated zest of 1 lemon

5 tbsp plain flour (all-purpose flour)

1 tsp fine sea salt

olive oil, for frying

To serve

4 brioche buns, or burger buns

tomato slices

lettuce leaves

mayonnaise

pickled vegetables, such as gherkins or onions

caramelized onions

1. Take the drained, pressed tofu and break it up in a large bowl with your hands until it has the same texture throughout.

2. Add the puréed sun-dried tomatoes and sriracha to the tofu and mix with a wooden spoon until the tofu is evenly coated and rosy in colour.

3. Add the herbs and shallot, and, using your hands, scrunch the mixture to ensure the herbs are well distributed.

4. Finally add the lemon zest, flour and salt, so the mix starts to come together in your hands.

5. Divide the mixture into 4 patties and leave to rest for 10 minutes.

6. Preheat the oven to 180°C fan/ 200°C/400°F/gas mark 6.

7. Heat a little olive oil in a frying pan (skillet), and fry the patties for 3–4 minutes on each side until golden brown. Try to fry them to the crispy, golden colour that you desire, as the baking stage firms up the centre and does not add much extra colour.

Transfer to a baking tray lined with baking parchment and cook in the oven for a further 20–25 minutes until the burgers are firm to the touch.

8. To assemble the burger, simply toast the burger buns lightly and build the burgers with tomato, lettuce, mayonnaise and pickles or caramelized onions of your choice; I love a slice of Gem lettuce, tomato and gherkin.

TWISTS

For more texture, you could add cooked kidney beans, black beans or chickpeas to the burger mix. Capers are also a great addition, for their pops of flavour. If you love fish, adding minced (ground) cod and prawns (shrimp) to the patty brings a sweetness, bounce and texture, too. Horseradish sauce, or tartare sauce, is an easy swap out for mayonnaise, if you like more sharpness.

These burgers are also great as sliders if you split the patty mix into 8 smaller burgers. The smaller patties crisp up better and so develop a firmer texture, too.

WALNUT TOFU SOBA NOODLE SALAD

As summer approaches, I transition from rice fiend to noodle enthusiast. Cool, firm noodles with plenty of bite, tossed in a variety of savoury, tangy, creamy sauces is what I crave. Noodle salads are made and enjoyed at a leisurely pace, simply perfect for summer dining. This mashed tofu sauce with plenty of crunchy vegetables makes a fantastic partner for the mighty buckwheat noodle, with walnuts doubling up on that rich nuttiness.

Serves 4

400g/14oz soba noodles

250g/12oz/2¾ cups crushed walnuts, plus extra to serve

6 tbsp brown sugar

240g/8½oz/scant 1¼ cups tahini

5 tbsp rice vinegar

4 tbsp light soy sauce

2½ tsp sea salt flakes

180ml/6fl oz/¾ cup water

300g/10½oz firm tofu, drained for 20 minutes, then mashed

4 spring onions (scallions), chopped into matchsticks

½ cucumber, sliced into fine batons

8 radishes, finely sliced

2 tbsp toasted sesame seeds

1. Cook the noodles according to the packet instructions (package directions), then rinse with cool water. Set aside.

2. In a large dry saucepan, toast the crushed walnuts for 2–3 minutes to release their oils, then transfer to a large bowl. Add the sugar, tahini, vinegar, soy sauce and salt and stir. It will be a thick paste, so stir in the water to loosen it throughout. Add the mashed tofu and stir to finish the dressing.

3. Toss the sauce loosely through the noodles, using tongs.

4. Add the spring onions, cucumber and radishes to the noodles and toss again.

5. Scatter with some extra toasted walnuts and the toasted sesame seeds before serving.

GANMODOKI TOFU PATTIES

Ganmodoki originally comes from *shojin ryori* – Japan's vegan cuisine created by Buddhist monks. These mini tofu cakes are pillowy, light and ever so moreish. When I first tried them at a street stall in Japan, I was told they were mock goose! Intriguing though that thought is, in reality these taste nothing like meat, but they are very satisfying patties. You find them in the convenience stores and supermarkets in Japan in little takeaway boxes, and they make a lovely on-the-go snack, ideal for a lunchbox treat or a picnic.

Makes 10

For the patties

250g/9oz firm tofu, drained for 20 minutes, pressed (see pages 14–15) and mashed

3 large dried shiitake mushrooms, soaked in hot water for 1–2 hours until fully hydrated, then drained and sliced into fine slivers

1 spring onion (scallion), finely sliced

¼ small carrot, grated

1 egg yolk, lightly beaten

1 tbsp white miso paste

25g/1oz/¼ cup panko crumbs

2 tbsp chopped coriander (cilantro)

sea salt flakes and freshly ground black pepper

vegetable oil, for oiling and frying

For the dipping sauce

1 tbsp chilli oil

1 tbsp rice vinegar

2 tsp caster sugar (superfine sugar)

1 tsp finely chopped red onion

1. First, take the mashed tofu, wrap it in kitchen paper (paper towels) and squeeze out any final drops of excess water. This is essential for firm patties. Put it in a bowl, add the mushrooms, spring onion and carrot and mix until evenly combined.

2. In a small bowl, stir together the egg yolk and miso paste until smooth, then add to the tofu mix. Finally, add the panko and coriander, season generously and lightly mix through again.

3. Shape into 10 golf ball-sized spheres, then flatten slightly on an oiled plate with your palm.

4. In a wide frying pan (skillet), heat up 1cm/½ inch of oil for a few minutes, until it starts to bubble. Using a spatula, lift each patty and place it in the pan for 2–3 minutes on each side until golden brown. Make sure there is at least 1cm/½ inch between each patty. (You may have to fry them in batches.)

5. Meanwhile, make the dipping sauce by mixing together all the ingredients in a small bowl and seasoning to taste.

6. Rest the patties on some kitchen paper to soak up any excess oil. They can be kept in a low oven until ready to serve, with the dipping sauce on the side.

TWISTS

This recipe is also great with chives instead of coriander, for a lighter, sweeter flavour.

MISO TOFU CELERY WONTONS

Making wontons brings back fond childhood memories of working in my father's restaurant. Every Sunday, I would be pressing minced (ground) pork and prawn (shrimp) fillings into my chubby palms and pleating the pastry quickly ahead of another busy lunch service, while my fingers slowly turned beetroot from the chilly climes of the basement kitchen.

As an adult, my love for wontons has been reborn, but I've always found tofu-based dumplings lacking in umami flavour and texture, missing the satisfying bite and fatty sweet richness of a compact, traditional meaty version. But this recipe delivers depth, firmness and freshness all at the same time. The miso brings a profundity of flavour without heaviness, celery adds a crunch and sharpness that keeps them light, mushrooms give a lovely chew, and the little bit of egg brings it all together to provide a bouncy texture that stays perky throughout cooking. These wontons are small, very light and delicate and should be served and enjoyed as soon as they are made.

Makes about 25

For the wontons

160g/5¾oz firm tofu, drained and pressed (see pages 14–15)

3 large dried shiitake mushrooms, soaked in hot water for 1–2 hours until fully hydrated, then drained and chopped into 1cm/½ inch dice

50g/1¾oz/½ cup celery sticks, chopped into 3mm/⅛ inch dice

1 thin spring onion (scallion) finely chopped

1½ tbsp toasted sesame oil

1 tsp light soy sauce

1 tbsp white miso paste

½ egg, lightly beaten

pinch of fine sea salt

2 pinches of freshly ground white pepper

25 wonton wrappers

For the dressing

1 long red chilli, finely chopped into 3mm/⅛ inch dice

4 tbsp rice vinegar

3 tbsp light soy sauce

1 tbsp toasted sesame oil

2 tsp finely chopped coriander (cilantro), half leaf, half stalk

1. Mince the tofu with your hands until it is an even crumb. Add the chopped mushrooms, celery and spring onion and give it a good stir.

2. In a small bowl, mix together the sesame oil, soy sauce and miso to create a runny paste and then add to the tofu mix, stirring gently to combine the flavours.

3. Finally add the egg, salt and pepper and leave for 20 minutes to set in the refrigerator.

4. Meanwhile, in a small bowl, mix all the dressing ingredients together.

5. Take a wonton wrapper and place it in your hand, angled like a kite or diamond shape. Put 1 tsp filling in the centre, then carefully fold the wrapper over the filling from bottom to top, to make a triangle. Now fold from left to right, to seal. Repeat to fill and shape all the wontons.

6. Bring a large saucepan of water to the boil, then reduce the heat to a low simmer. Add 6–7 wontons at a time, cooking gently for 3 minutes. As the filling of the wontons is largely cooked already, they do not need long to cook at all. Lift out with a slotted spoon and place on kitchen paper (paper towels) to drain. Repeat to cook all the wontons. It is easy to overcook wontons, so take care with the cooking time and lift them out quickly. (If the water is too vigorously boiling, the dumplings can break up.)

7. Place the cooked wontons on a platter and spoon over the dressing, serving some more on the side as a dipping sauce.

PEI PA TOFU

This makes a great centrepiece. I admit, it's a little fiddly – given the many stages – but it's an easy recipe to prepare in advance. Mashed tofu with seasonings and other ingredients are formed into little dumplings using a ceramic spoon, steamed or pan-fried and served with a savoury sauce. The *pei pa* name refers to a pear-shaped Chinese musical instrument, the lute that the tofu shapes (vaguely) resemble. You can choose either to steam or to fry this dish.

Serves 4

For the tofu

300g/10½oz firm tofu, drained and pressed (see pages 14–15)

1 dried shiitake mushroom, soaked in water for 1–2 hours until fully hydrated, then drained and diced

50g/1¾oz/1 cup peeled and julienned carrots

1 egg white

3 tbsp cornflour (corn starch), plus 3 tbsp extra (optional) for frying

1 tbsp chopped spring onions (scallions), or chives

1 tbsp chopped coriander (cilantro) leaves, plus extra to serve

2 tsp light soy sauce

1 tsp caster sugar (superfine sugar)

¼ tsp fine sea salt

½ tsp freshly ground white pepper

vegetable oil, for greasing and (optional) deep-frying

50g/1¾oz/¼ cup rice flour (optional), for frying

spinach, kale or broccoli, to serve

For the sauce

1 tsp vegetable oil

2 garlic cloves, finely minced

1 tbsp Shaoxing rice wine

1 tbsp oyster sauce or mushroom sauce

½ tsp caster sugar (superfine sugar)

2 tsp light soy sauce

¼ tsp dark soy sauce

1 tsp cornflour (corn starch)

1. Mash the drained tofu with a fork, then place in a sieve to squeeze out any more excess liquid. (Soft or silken tofu will not work in this recipe.)

2. Place the tofu, mushroom, carrots and egg white into a food processor and pulse until you have a paste consistency. Stir in the cornflour, spring onions and coriander leaves and mix until the paste is smooth. Then add the soy sauce, sugar, salt and pepper to the mix.

3. Lightly brush a Chinese ceramic soup spoon with vegetable oil, then, using your hands, mould the paste into the spoon, to create the shape of the *pei pa*.

4. If you're steaming the dish, gently slide the tofu dumpling off the spoon and onto a steaming basket. Keep doing this until all the mixture is used up. Place the *pei pa* tofu in the steamer and steam over a high heat for 6–7 minutes. When removing the plate from the steamer, reserve the steaming liquid from the plate (and pan) for use in the sauce, as it is full of flavour.

5. If you are not eating this dish immediately, wrap the tofu and keep in the refrigerator until you're ready to finish the dish.

6. If you are frying the *pei pa*, mix the rice flour with the extra 3 tbsp cornflour in a large bowl. Warm 5cm/2 inches of oil for frying in a deep saucepan; the oil should reach no more than one-third of the way up the sides of the pan. Coat the *pei pa* with the flour mix, then deep-fry in batches – being careful not to crowd the pan – until golden brown on all sides. Remove from the oil with a slotted spoon and place on kitchen paper, then continue to cook the subsequent batches.

7. For the sauce, heat the oil in a pan, add the garlic and stir-fry briefly. Pour in 250ml/9fl oz/1 cup of the reserved steaming liquid followed by the rest of the ingredients for the sauce, except the cornflour. Bring to a simmer. To thicken the sauce, mix the cornflour with 1 tbsp water in a small bowl and pour into the simmering sauce.

8. To serve, arrange the *pei pa* tofu on a platter on a bed of wilted spinach, kale, or broccoli, then pour the sauce on top and enjoy immediately, scattered with chopped coriander.

SILKEN TOFU

Silken tofu requires no pressing, hardly any draining and minimum intervention to make it taste fantastic. I always have a box of silken tofu in the refrigerator, ready to be loaded with various condiments and toppings, or added to noodle soup for a lazy dinner.

I know this sounds dramatic, but silken tofu is probably the most misunderstood of all tofu. Usually found in cardboard cartons, or sometimes in trays of water, it has a pannacotta-style texture and should really carry the warning sign: *'Do not stir-fry!'* If you have ever bought this kind of tofu and tried to move it around quickly in a pan, you will know that you end up with a kind of tofu slurry that is not going to win you any prizes. To ace silken tofu, you need to know about these three tasty applications:

1. SOUPS
Silken tofu's feather-light texture allows it to float effortlessly in silky soups and is particularly welcome in spicy broths and stews, where it brings a cool creaminess to calm the palate.

2. FULLY LOADED
Statuesque and striking: load up a block of silken tofu with bold flavours and crunchy ingredients. Think of the silken tofu itself here as a canvas on which to paint your favourite flavours and textures; silken tofu loves deep soy sauces, sharp vinegars and chilli spice as well as crunchy and crispy textures.

3. DESSERTS
Embrace the creamy body of silken tofu and fold it into your desserts, where it achieves silky textures simply, without the richness of cream. You'll find plenty of recipes in the Sweet Tofu chapter (see page 128).

FULLY LOADED SPICY XI'AN COLD TOFU

This recipe is, by far, the easiest dish in this book; but more than that, the effort-to-results ratio is embarrassingly high. This is the dish I roll out on desperate evenings, when I am so hungry and tired that I can't even muster up the energy to heat a pan, yet need something quick and satisfying. With this dish at my fingertips I have staved off many a takeaway order.

Traditionally – and perhaps surprisingly – this is based on a breakfast dish in China, served with hot steamed rice. The tofu is chilled and cool like ricotta, but laced with zingy-hot, salty and sour flavours and finished with crunchy, mouth-popping toppings. I love it with plain rice or noodles, to soak up all those tantalizing flavours.

Serves 2 as a main course, or 4 as a side dish

For the tofu

300g/10½oz silken tofu block, drained for 20 minutes

1 tsp Sichuan preserved pickled vegetables (find this in Asian stores in jars or packets)

1 spring onion (scallion), finely sliced

1 tbsp Chinkiang vinegar

2 tsp light soy sauce

2 tbsp Chinese chilli oil with sediment

1 tsp toasted sesame oil

rice, or salads, to serve (optional)

For the topping (choose just one, or as many as you like)

fried red-skinned peanuts, or soya beans

Bombay mix

crisp fried garlic or onions

toasted seeds

1. Simply pop the silken tofu out of its box or tray, there's no need to press it. Place in a small deep bowl (for people to share) and top with the Sichuan preserved vegetables and spring onion.

2. In another small bowl, mix together the vinegar, soy sauce, chilli oil and sesame oil and pour on top of the tofu.

3. Finish with something crunchy, such as fried peanuts, Bombay mix, crispy garlic or onions or toasted seeds.

4. You can eat this with rice as I do, but it's also great as a summer dish, with salads.

TWISTS

You can quickly and easily adapt the toppings here to suit the ingredients you have at home; silken tofu loves sharp deep flavours, so have a look in your cupboards to see what you have that fits this profile. I have used capers, chopped gherkins and pickled onions for sharpness; Worcestershire sauce, balsamic vinegar or date molasses for sweet acidity; and for crunch, cashew nuts and pine nuts work a treat.

STEAMED SILKEN TOFU WITH ENOKI MUSHROOMS & SWEET SOY

Here is a fully loaded silken tofu dish that is warming, with delicate flavours. Growing up in a Cantonese family, a steamed fish was always on the table. Simply dressed with sweet soy sauce, ginger and spring onions, it was comforting and nutritious, allowing all the fresh natural flavours to sing. With really fresh tofu, I recommend the same treatment. If you have made your own tofu (see page 22), or want to enjoy silken tofu simply, this is a dish that you can easily experiment with. The final touch is a dash of hot sizzling oil, just before serving, to release the flavours of the spring onions and ginger. Perfect with steamed rice and stir-fried greens.

Serves 2 as a main course, or 4 as part of a sharing meal

150g/5½oz silken tofu block, drained for 20 minutes, or Home-made Tofu (see page 22)

1 spring onion (scallion), finely sliced into small matchsticks

thumb of fresh ginger, peeled and finely sliced into small matchsticks

2 tbsp light muscovado sugar

1 tbsp Shaoxing rice wine

2 tbsp dark soy sauce

pinch of freshly ground white pepper

1 tbsp toasted sesame oil

2 tbsp chopped coriander (cilantro)

handful of enoki mushrooms

2 tbsp olive oil

steamed rice and stir-fried greens, to serve

1. Take a deep heatproof bowl (for people to share) and place the tofu block inside, allowing about 2cm/¾ inch of space around the tofu. Sprinkle half the spring onion and ginger on top.

2. In a separate bowl, mix together the sugar, Shaoxing wine and soy sauce, then pour the mixture over the tofu.

3. Sprinkle with a pinch of ground white pepper, the sesame oil and chopped coriander. Finally, place the enoki mushrooms around the tofu.

4. Steam the bowl for 12–15 minutes until all the ingredients are heated through.

5. When ready to serve, heat the olive oil in a small saucepan until bubbling hot. Sprinkle the rest of the ginger and spring onions on top of the tofu and immediately follow with the hot oil. It will sizzle!

TWISTS

You can vary the toppings for this tofu easily; go for mild-tasting vegetables such as aubergines (eggplant), pak choi (bok choy), Chinese cabbage and mushrooms, that can carry the seasonings well. For those who enjoy meat, a small amount of minced (ground) pork on top of the tofu releases a richness into the dish. Chopped prawns (shrimp) could also be added, for delicate sweetness and added texture.

HOT & SOUR SOUP

Thick but silky, spicy yet sour; an invigorating bowl for the senses. A mainstay of Chinese menus, I love the way this soup wakes up your tastebuds at the start of a meal. Getting it right is not easy. It is a dish predicated on balance, and striking the exact ratio of salty, sour, sweet and spicy flavours guarantees deep satisfaction. If you are too heavy-handed with any one flavour, it topples, so taste as you add each ingredient, to build up the exciting flavour journey.

A happy home for lots of finely sliced vegetables, this soup is a versatile dish for lunch or dinner. The creamy tofu cubes calm the palate, while stimulating slurps of citrus, spice and umami follow.

Serves 4

1.5 litres/2¾ pints/1.6 quarts vegetable stock or dashi (see pages 27–8)

6 large dried shiitake mushrooms, soaked for 1–2 hours until fully hydrated, then drained and finely sliced

100g/3½oz/¾ cup bamboo shoots, sliced into thin matchsticks (optional)

100ml/3½fl oz/scant ½ cup rice vinegar, or to taste

70ml/2½fl oz/generous ¼ cup light soy sauce

2 tsp caster sugar (superfine sugar)

2 tsp grated fresh ginger

1½–2 tsp chilli garlic sauce from a jar, or to taste

30g/1oz/2 tbsp cornflour (corn starch)

250g/9oz silken tofu, cut into 1cm/½ inch cubes

2 tsp toasted sesame oil

2 large eggs, lightly beaten

½ tsp fine sea salt

½ tsp freshly ground white pepper

4 spring onions (scallions), finely sliced

1 large red chilli (not too hot), deseeded and finely sliced

1. Heat up the stock in a saucepan and add the mushrooms, bamboo shoots, vinegar, soy sauce, sugar, ginger and chilli garlic sauce. Simmer for 3–4 minutes, then reduce the heat to low.

2. In a small bowl, mix the cornflour with 4 tbsp of water and stir until smooth, then add to the pan; the soup will slowly thicken.

3. Add the tofu and sesame oil.

4. Swirl the soup so there is some movement in the pan. Drizzle in the eggs from a height to create ribbons, then turn off the heat.

5. Add the salt and pepper, then taste; if you like it more sour, add more rice vinegar, and if you like it spicier, add more chilli garlic sauce. The balance of this dish is down to personal taste.

6. Before serving, sprinkle with the spring onions and red chilli.

TWISTS

Adding prawns (shrimp) with their shells on adds extra umami flavour to this soup, while slices of roast ham are a quick way to add flavour and texture, too. A mix of wild mushrooms to soak up the silky soup also works well. Smoked tofu could be used instead of silken tofu, for a deeper flavour.

SOYA MILK AND TOFU MISO SOUP

This creamy number (photographed on the previous page) is inspired by clam chowders and fish pie mixes, in which milk is infused with herbs and deep flavours to become a luxurious liquor… but in this case, it's soya milk and miso. The tangy, umami-rich paste brings richness to the milk, as well as a light caramel colour as it simmers and thickens. Quick and filling, this makes a speedy lunch or an easy base to which to add other tasty ingredients.

Serves 4

1 small leek, finely sliced

2 tbsp vegetable oil

600ml/1 pint/2½ cups unsweetened soya milk

6 tbsp white miso paste

500ml/18fl oz/generous 2 cups hot water

400g/14oz silken tofu, sliced into cubes

2 spring onions (scallions), finely sliced

1 tsp toasted sesame oil

1. In a frying pan, gently sauté the leek in the oil over a low heat for 3–4 minutes, until softened. Add the soya milk and set aside to allow the flavours to infuse.

2. Spoon 3 tbsp of the infused milk into a small cup and mix in the miso paste until smooth. Pour the miso mixture back into the pan. Add the hot water gradually, stirring and tasting as you go; the amount you will need depends on how strong you like your miso soup. Turn off the heat and add the silken tofu.

3. Divide between 4 bowls. Top with the spring onions and a couple of drops of sesame oil, then serve.

TWISTS

Instead of leeks, you could try using red onions to bring sweetness. The world's your oyster when it comes to additional toppings; just choose those ingredients with textures that contrast with the soft white tofu cubes, such as seafood – try prawns (shrimp), crayfish or clams – or, to make *tonjiru* miso soup, slices of pork belly.

YUDOFU

For the tofu

500ml/18fl oz/2 generous cups dashi (see pages 27–8)

1 tbsp sake

pinch of fine sea salt

250g/9oz freshly made tofu (see page 22), or silken tofu, cut into 2.5cm/1 inch blocks

spring onions, finely sliced, to serve

For the dressing

60ml/4 tbsp light soy sauce

1 tbsp sake

1 tsp mirin

1 tsp toasted sesame seeds

½ tsp caster sugar (superfine sugar)

This is a super-simple way to enjoy freshly made tofu, or a simple block of silken tofu, as its simplicity is designed to really hone in on its delicate flavours. *Yudofu* simply translates as 'hot tofu' in Japanese and it can be made in minutes with just a couple of storecupboard ingredients. The warm tofu is drizzled with a sweet soy-and-dashi-based sauce. Great as a side dish for a wider meal.

1. Make the dressing by combining all the ingredients and mixing until the sugar dissolves. Lightly simmer in a small saucepan for 2 minutes to reduce the sake.

2. Warm the dashi for the tofu in a heavy-based saucepan. Add the sake and salt and simmer for 1 minute, then add the tofu and simmer for 2 minutes more.

3. Serve immediately, sprinkled with the spring onions, with the dressing on the side for dipping.

SILKEN TOFU SOUP WITH PICKLED MUSTARD GREENS

This dish is inspired by the Sichuanese dish *suan cai yu*, a spicy-sour broth made with pickled Chinese mustard greens – that you can find in Asian stores – and poached white fish, usually catfish or tilapia. It is so comforting on a cold day: spicy, sour, nourishing, light and zingy. Silken tofu is a great swap for fish here, to calm the heat in every mouthful. Traditionally, it is eaten as a dish with rice, but I love it as a bright and punchy soup starter too. I have included a traditional spicy oil topping, which you will want if you are enjoying this dish with rice, as it really super-charges the flavours.

Serves 4

For the soup

300g/10½oz silken tofu

2 tbsp vegetable oil

3 spring onions (scallions), finely sliced, plus extra to serve

4 garlic cloves, minced

10g/¼oz/2 tsp fresh ginger, minced

2 dried chillies

1–1½ tbsp chilli bean paste (*doban jiang*), to taste

250g/9oz Sichuan pickled mustard greens, sliced if the bulbs are large

2 tbsp chopped jalapeño chillies, or to taste

1 tbsp Shaoxing rice wine,

800ml/1½ pints/3¼ cups vegetable, fish or chicken stock, or dashi (see pages 27–8)

2 tsp caster sugar (superfine sugar)

½ tsp fine sea salt, or to taste

¼ tsp freshly ground white pepper, or to taste

squeeze of lemon juice (optional)

For the spicy topping (if serving with rice)

2 tbsp olive oil

1 tsp Sichuan peppercorns

1 tbsp chilli bean paste (*doban jiang*)

1. First, drain and slice the tofu into rough cubes. This is a rustic dish, so don't worry about irregular pieces. Cover and set aside.

2. Next, prepare a large wok or casserole pan for the soup base. Heat the oil over medium heat until warm, and before it gets smoking hot, add the spring onions, garlic, ginger and dried chillies and cook for 2 minutes, stirring frequently.

3. Add the chilli bean paste and stir around to mingle with the spices. Add the chopped mustard greens and jalapeños and stir-fry for a further 3 minutes. Add the Shaoxing wine and stir again. Pour in all the stock and bring to a simmer for 5 minutes, then take the pickles out and place them in a large serving bowl.

4. Return the rest of the pan of flavoured stock to the boil, add the sugar, salt and white pepper and mix well until dissolved. Taste the broth; it should be salty, sour and spicy. If you'd like it to be spicier, add more white pepper; more salty, add more salt; or more sour, add a few more jalapeños or even a squeeze of lemon juice. Reduce the heat and add the tofu gently to the pan with a slotted spoon. Simmer for 30 seconds as the tofu warms through, then spoon the soup into the serving bowl on top of the pickles.

5. For the spicy topping, in a small frying pan, warm up the oil and add the Sichuan peppercorns and chilli bean paste. Once the oil is red and the peppercorns become dark, use a fine sieve to remove them, then pour the flavoured oil over the silken tofu.

6. Scatter with some more spring onions and serve hot as a soup, or enjoy with rice.

TWISTS

Try this dish with added white fish for the full original experience. For this, season bite-sized pieces of white fish fillet with fine sea salt, freshly ground white pepper and a dash of Shaoxing rice wine, then coat with a dusting of potato flour for a silky texture, before adding to the soup to poach when the stock is bubbling hot.

SAPPORO MISO RAMEN WITH TOFU, SOY EGGS & CORN

Hokkaido – Japan's most northerly island – is home to a wonderful cuisine rich in local produce, especially dairy. Their ramen is topped with local butter and their buns with cream cheese. The bakeries are dangerously good and the convenience stores are stocked with creamy Hokkaido milk and ice cream. Hokkaido ramen uses miso in its broth, either on its own or together with pork broth as is traditional. Sometimes the miso is mixed with seafood stock or soya milk, too, which creates a lightness that is still deep in umami but much less rich. This dish is inspired by the alleys of miso ramen bars I love in Sapporo. The local butter on top is the icing on the cake.

Serves 4

For the broth and noodles

300–350g/10½–12oz dried ramen noodles

1.5 litres/2¾ pints/1.6 quarts dashi (see pages 27–8) or water

200g/7oz/¾ cup white miso paste

4 tbsp toasted sesame oil

For the toppings

150ml/5fl oz/⅔ cup light soy sauce

100ml/3½fl oz/scant ½ cup mirin

4 eggs, hard-boiled and peeled

600g/1lb 5oz silken tofu

8 tbsp sweetcorn (corn), drained if canned or steamed if frozen

knob of salted butter (optional)

4 tbsp finely chopped chives

1. First, make the soy eggs topping. Mix the soy sauce and mirin in a bowl and immerse the peeled eggs in the liquid for 1 hour.

2. Cook the ramen noodles according to the packet instructions (package directions), then rinse and drain.

3. To make the broth, boil the dashi or water in a large saucepan. Meanwhile, mix the miso paste and sesame oil in a bowl, before pouring it into the hot liquid.

4. Slice the tofu into thick slabs and simmer in the hot broth for 30 seconds.

5. Assemble the bowls of ramen, starting with the noodles, then the hot miso broth, and topping with the soy egg, tofu and corn.

6. Finish the dish with the butter, if using, and chives.

TWISTS

Swap the dashi or water for a fish or chicken stock for a deeper flavour. Consider any toppings you like, including mushrooms, courgettes (zucchini), chicken or bacon, as well as other forms of tofu including crispy tofu (see page 30) and *aburaage* deep-fried tofu (see page 10).

KOREAN TOFU STEW

This kimchi-spiced tofu stew is a real Korean cuisine mainstay. Traditionally served in a dramatic iron hotpot or stone pot, it arrives bubbling like a cauldron, and looks much spicier than it really is. Called *sundubu-jigae* ('soft tofu stew'), it is a deeply flavoured broth that weaves around silken tofu, other chunky ingredients such as kimchi, and seafood such as oysters and prawns. Enjoy it with white rice and other crunchy side dishes, such as stir-fried beansprouts.

Serves 4

2 tbsp Korean chilli flakes (*gochugaru*)

2 tbsp vegetable oil

2 tsp finely chopped or grated garlic

2 tsp light soy sauce

800ml/1¼ pints/3½ cups vegetable stock or dashi (see pages 27–8)

1 tsp sea salt flakes

4 eggs

700g/1lb 9oz silken tofu, cut into rough chunks

100g/3½oz/1½ cups oyster mushrooms or shimeji mushrooms

4 dried shiitake mushrooms, soaked for 1–2 hours until fully hydrated, then drained and finely sliced

150g/5½oz/1½ cups kimchi

2 spring onions (scallions), finely sliced on the diagonal

1 tbsp toasted sesame oil

rice, to serve

1. In a large, heavy-based saucepan, heat the Korean chilli flakes with the vegetable oil for 1 minute, then add the garlic and soy sauce.

2. Pour the stock into the pan and heat up for 2–3 minutes, then add the salt.

3. Gently crack the eggs one at a time into the pan to lightly poach them for 3 minutes, then add the tofu and all the mushrooms and simmer for a further 3 minutes. Finally add the kimchi.

4. Sprinkle the spring onions and toasted sesame oil on top, then serve with steamed rice.

TWISTS

Try swapping the vegetable stock for fish stock and adding seafood such as clams and prawns (shrimp). Slices of bacon are also popular, for a richer broth.

CANTONESE EGG TOFU & PAK CHOI

These little golden coins of egg tofu are affectionately also known as 'vegetarian scallops' for their tender, rich sweetness and mini medallion shape. Typically served on top of simple stir-fried vegetables, they bring a touch of luxury to humble greens. Handling egg tofu needs a little practice; thankfully, it is usually packed in cylinder tubes, making it easier to slice. It is great on top of greens such as broccoli, gai lan or pak choi.

Chinese egg tofu is a type of silken tofu, made in a similar way to tofu; eggs are mixed into soya milk before a coagulant is added to set the tofu.

Serves 3–4 as a side dish

150g/5½oz packet (package) egg tofu

50g/1¾oz/scant ½ cup cornflour (corn starch), plus 1 tsp extra for the sauce

5 tbsp vegetable oil

3 garlic cloves, finely sliced

4 heads of pak choi (bok choy), quartered lengthways

2 tbsp mushroom sauce or oyster sauce

50ml/1¾fl oz/scant ¼ cup water

1. Preheat the oven to 160°C fan/180°C/350°F/gas mark 4.

2. Slice open the tofu packet and cut the egg tofu into 1.5cm/½ inch discs. Carefully lay them on a tray with the 50g/1¾oz/scant ½ cup cornflour and flip them over, so they are coated on both sides.

3. Heat 3 tbsp of the oil in a frying pan (skillet) until bubbling hot, then, one by one, fry each disc of tofu. The tofu should sizzle when hitting the pan, or else the oil is not hot enough. After 90 seconds, flip the pieces over so that both sides lightly crisp. Keep them warm in the oven while you prepare the vegetables.

4. In a frying pan, heat the remaining oil and stir-fry the garlic for 2 minutes before adding the pak choi. Stir-fry for a further 4–5 minutes until the pak choi has softened. Set aside.

5. Place a small saucepan over a low heat. Add the mushroom or oyster sauce, the water and the 1 tsp cornflour until it thickens into a silky sauce.

6. Lay the pak choi on a plate, place the golden discs of tofu on top and pour the sauce over the whole thing for a glossy, lacquered finish.

TWISTS

For a crispier and richer-tasting egg tofu, dip the discs in lightly beaten egg before you coat it in cornflour to fry.

JAPANESE TOFU SALAD WITH SESAME CITRUS DRESSING

This classic dish is often part of a wider Japanese meal, bringing balance and lightness to the table, much in the same way as a garden salad would in a Western meal. With a trusty box of silken tofu in the refrigerator, you can easily put this together with bits from your salad drawer. I like it for lunch with bread, or to accompany a heavier noodle or rice dish in the evening.

Serves 2

For the salad

80g/2¾oz/2½ packed cups mixed lettuce leaves, washed and dried

8 baby tomatoes, halved

50g/1¾oz/scant ½ cup sweetcorn (corn)

1 tbsp dried wakame seaweed, soaked in water, then drained (optional)

250g/9oz block silken tofu, drained

For the dressing

1 tbsp light soy sauce

1 tbsp toasted sesame oil

1 tbsp mirin

1 tbsp rice vinegar

1 tbsp water

1 tsp yuzu juice, or lemon juice

⅛ tsp fine sea salt

½ tbsp toasted sesame seeds

1. First make the dressing by combining all the liquid ingredients in a small bowl, then adding the salt and toasted sesame seeds.

2. Fill a large serving bowl with the mixed lettuce leaves and add the baby tomatoes, sweetcorn and wakame.

3. Slice the tofu block carefully into 1cm/½ inch cubes and place over the vegetables.

4. Drizzle some of the dressing evenly over the salad, serving the rest on the side.

TWISTS

Add new textures and flavours to this classic salad, such as chopped egg, shredded chicken breast, avocado, crayfish or prawns (shrimp).

FERMENTED TOFU

Fermented tofu is the blue cheese of Asia: you will either love it or hate it. It is so deep in umami that it smacks you around the chops, and so tangy that it makes your tongue ache. It's not for everyone, but I love it.

There are a few types of fermented tofu: white, red and spicy are the most common. Essentially they are small, soft cubes of tofu that have been fermented, then marinated in a brine of various ingredients, and are ready to eat once they reach a feta cheese-like, fudgy texture.

The heady world of fermented tofu is super-easy for us home cooks to employ in our food. All the work is already done for you and it is available from all Asian stores in ceramic pots (that double up well as plant pots, once retired). Used most commonly as a sauce or marinade, fermented tofu has a heavy kick – a little goes a long way – but is so balanced that you don't need to add any extra seasoning. It is a ready-to-go sauce that needs nothing else but fresh ingredients.

If you love pungent flavours such as red wine, aged cheese and kimchi, then I am confident that you will love fermented tofu, as I do. Just a whiff of its distinctive aroma makes my mouth water. If you develop a real taste for it, making your own is surprisingly simple (see page 25).

STIR-FRIED SPINACH WITH WHITE FERMENTED TOFU

Probably the easiest sauce ever for stir-frying greens. White fermented tofu, which you can find in jars in most Asian stores, is a life-saver when you are short on time. The delicate jade sauce pools prettily around the vegetables and has a creamy, savoury flavour that is still a little tangy from the fermentation. I use this in so much of my cooking; a super-versatile, gentle umami booster in a jar, it's great with leafy green vegetables such as pak choi (bok choy), cavolo nero, chard, morning glory (*tung choi*) and even celery leaves.

Serves 2–3 as a side dish

3 tbsp vegetable oil

4 garlic cloves, finely sliced

1 large red chilli, finely sliced, plus extra to serve

500g/1lb 2oz spinach leaves

100g/3½oz/4 cubes white fermented tofu

1. In a large frying pan (skillet) or wok, heat up the oil for 2–3 minutes, then add the garlic and chilli and fry for 1 minute.

2. Add the spinach leaves in batches, putting more in the pan as the earlier batches wilt down.

3. Meanwhile, put the tofu into a small bowl and break the cubes up into a paste with a spoon.

4. Once all the spinach leaves are in the pan and starting to wilt, add the tofu paste and stir-fry for 2–3 minutes.

5. Scatter with some extra red chilli before serving.

RED FERMENTED TOFU CAULIFLOWER STEAKS

This roasted cauliflower makes for an impressive main dish, with unbelievably low levels of effort. The long-fermented red tofu does all the hard work for you, so it's as easy as buttering toast. The key to getting this dish right is to steam the cauliflower before roasting it, to ensure the steaks remain juicy. The long, winey notes of red fermented tofu are dreamy and stand up well against the woody cauliflower. Delicious with mashed potato, rice, or a light chopped salad.

Serves 4

2 medium cauliflowers

4 tbsp olive oil

½ tsp freshly ground black pepper

200g/7oz/about 6 cubes red fermented tofu, drained

3 garlic cloves, finely chopped or grated

toasted sesame seeds, to serve

steamed noodles or rice, or chopped salad, to serve

1. Preheat the oven to 180°C fan/200°C/400°F/gas mark 6.

2. Trim the bases from the cauliflowers, then cut them straight through the middle into 2.5cm/1 inch thick steaks.

3. Trim off the leaves. Lay the cauliflower steaks on a baking tray lined with enough foil to seal over the top as well.

4. Rub the oil all over the cauliflower steaks, sprinkle with the pepper and seal up the foil. Bake/steam in the oven for 15 minutes. Unwrap the foil and bake for a further 15 minutes. The cauliflower steaks will start to become golden and crispy around the edges.

5. In a bowl, mix the tofu cubes and garlic until you have a smooth sauce. Brush or spread this mixture over the top of the cauliflower steaks, then roast for a further 10 minutes until crispy and golden.

6. Top with toasted sesame seeds to finish, then serve with steamed noodles or rice, or a chopped salad.

TWISTS

Try this fermented tofu topping when baking other dense vegetables, such as butternut squash and swede (rutabaga). A light spread of red fermented tofu is also a great umami booster on gamey red meats.

NOODLE HOTPOT WITH RED FERMENTED TOFU

Slow cooking with red fermented tofu fills the air with a heady aroma that lingers. It reminds me nostalgically of making coq au vin weekly in my first cooking job in the French Alps, more than a decade ago. The dark, winey, beany flavours are sweet, deep and addictively pungent. This has rich tones of duck pâté or plummy wine; nothing like you might expect from tofu! Traditionally, this red fermented tofu sauce is enjoyed in China in braised dishes of duck and other gamey meats, but in this plant-based recipe, the heavy burgundy tones deliver a mighty 'meaty' – but meatless – effect.

This hotpot can take a lot of ingredients, so choose those that have bite and chew: glass noodles, shiitake mushrooms, prawns (shrimp) and beancurd rolls, as well as spongy vegetables such as pak choi, oyster mushrooms and courgettes (zucchini) to soak up the maroon liquor. Serve with plenty of steamed rice.

Serves 4

100g/3½oz dried tofu sticks, soaked in hot water for 30 minutes, then drained

2 tbsp vegetable oil

2 spring onions (scallions), finely sliced

1 garlic clove, finely sliced

thumb of fresh ginger, peeled and finely chopped or grated

200g/7oz/4 large cubes red fermented tofu, with 4 tbsp liquor from the jar

1 litre/1¾ pints/1 quart hot water

50g/1¾oz/generous ½ cup shiitake mushrooms

2 heads of pak choi (bok choy), quartered lengthways

50g/1¾oz glass noodles, soaked in hot water according to the packet instructions (package directions), then drained

handful of coriander (cilantro) leaves

steamed rice, to serve

1. Cut the rehydrated tofu sticks into 5cm/2 inch pieces with kitchen scissors. Set aside.

2. In a heavy-based casserole, or large saucepan, heat up the vegetable oil, then add the spring onions, garlic and ginger. Sauté for 3 minutes, then add the rehydrated tofu pieces.

3. In a small bowl, using a fork, mash the fermented tofu cubes and their liquor to a paste, then gradually mix in the hot water. Pour it into the pan. The ingredients will start to soak up the sauce immediately.

4. Add the mushrooms and pak choi, then cover and simmer over a low heat for 15 minutes, stirring halfway through to ensure nothing is sticking to the pan.

5. Add the cooked glass noodles for the last 5 minutes of cooking; it is important that they do not overcook so that they keep their bite.

6. Scatter with coriander, then serve with steamed rice.

TRIPLE TOFU BANH MI WITH QUICK PICKLES

The French-Vietnamese filled baguette – the banh mi – for me, really is the perfect sandwich. Ambitiously, this one takes on all six flavours in every bite: sweet, salty, spicy, sour, bitter and umami are all present and correct. Crunchy on the outside, juicy and soft on the inside, with plenty of chew and crunch, this is no ordinary sandwich; sharp, spicy, rich, it vigorously stimulates your every sense, bite after bite.

Sadly, I often find vegetarian versions of banh mi a bit lacking. While pleasant, they often miss the mark when it comes to hitting those complex flavour notes and textures. Traditionally, a banh mi's meaty filling is paired with a thick meat pâté, and, in my recipe, I've created its plant-based match. Crispy tofu is wrapped alongside sharp crunchy pickles, then cushioned with a generous, velvety spread of fermented red tofu, lending its deep richness. A mustardy silken tofu sauce adds lightness. Let's make veggie banh mi that will never disappoint again.

Makes 4 deeply filled baguettes

For the quick carrot pickle (optional)

110ml/3½fl oz/scant ½ cup rice vinegar, or white wine vinegar

100g/3½oz/½ cup caster sugar (superfine sugar)

1 star anise

1 tsp sea salt flakes

3 carrots, peeled and julienned

For the sauce and tofu pâté

200g/7oz silken tofu

1½ tbsp wholegrain mustard

½ tsp finely grated lime zest

large pinch of sea salt flakes

large pinch of freshly ground black pepper

200g/7oz/4 large cubes red fermented tofu, drained

For the crispy tofu

150g/5½oz/scant 1¼ cups cornflour (corn starch)

400g/14oz firm tofu, cut into 8 even slabs (2 pieces per baguette)

3 tbsp vegetable oil

For the baguettes

4 crusty baguettes

2 handfuls of coriander (cilantro), roughly chopped

2 red chillies, finely sliced on an angle

finely sliced pickled gherkins and onions, or quick carrot pickle (see above)

1. First make the pickle, if using. In a small saucepan, bring the vinegar, sugar, star anise and salt to the boil, then allow to cool. Place the carrots in a large bowl and pour the liquid over. Allow to sit for 30–60 minutes before draining. If you are using ready-made pickles, you can obviously skip to the next step.

2. To make the creamy sauce, break down the silken tofu in a small bowl until totally smooth using a spoon, then add the mustard, lime zest, salt and pepper. Set aside.

3. To prepare the fermented tofu pâté, simply break up the cubes from the jar in a separate bowl until you have a smooth paste.

4. Put the cornflour in a shallow dish. Coat the firm tofu in the cornflour on all sides. Heat the oil in a large frying pan (skillet) and fry the tofu pieces until golden on all sides. Keep these warm in a low oven while you get the rest of the ingredients ready.

5. Now to make the sandwich, warm up the baguettes in a medium-low oven, so that they are crispy and warm on the outside and fluffy on the inside, and slice along one long side of each, ready to be stuffed.

6. When ready to serve, spread the fermented tofu paste generously on both inner sides of the bread. Stuff each sandwich with the coriander, chillies and pickles, then finally the crispy tofu. Finish with a drizzle of the silken tofu sauce. Enjoy immediately.

TWISTS

If you don't have fermented tofu to hand, a good mushroom pâté can also work well. The crispy tofu can be replaced with oily fish such as fried salmon or mackerel, or fatty meats such as roast pork.

DRIED & FRIED TOFU

Dried and fried tofu are prepared very differently, but they are gathered together here in this section because they provide a very similar mouthfeel once cooked: they are both chewy and great for those who want some bite from tofu. When cooking vegetarian dishes, I rely on dried and fried tofu to provide that firm resistant texture that I often crave.

Dried tofu – which often goes by its (to me) less appetizing alternative names of 'tofu skins' or 'bean curd sticks' – is different from fresh tofu not only in texture but also in flavour. Dried tofu is the skin that forms on the top of soya milk, once the milk has been left to cool (much as you would expect on cow's milk), which is skimmed off, then hung up to dry like sheets in a laundry. This dried tofu is more intense in flavour than fresh tofu, in the same way that cream is richer than milk. Dried tofu therefore has a deep sweetness that is much more intense than fresh tofu, and is considered a delicacy in Chinese cuisine.

Dried tofu is a fantastic pantry staple that hydrates into a total protein-rich superstar in 20–30 minutes, so I always have plenty on standby to make a quick meal. You can find it in the dried soup ingredients section of Asian stores, in sheets, sticks or knot shapes, and they last for years, so stock up! In Japanese cuisine, it is called *yuba*. Once you have rehydrated it, use it within a day.

Fried tofu is found in the chilled or frozen section of Asian stores in large packets. There are two major types of deep-fried tofu: firstly, there are large tofu puffs that are spongy and elastic; these are both popular in Chinese dishes and also in Japanese cuisine, where they are known as *atsuage*. These are fairly easy to make at home (see page 26). Secondly, there is a type of fried tofu called *aburaage* in Japanese; these are thin little pillowcases of fried tofu that can be sliced and enjoyed as a soup topping or opened up and filled with rice (see pages 124–125).

Fried tofu has a supremely satisfying texture – comparable to biting into focaccia, fresh doughnuts or profiteroles – and is just as addictive!

SWEET & STICKY
TOFU KNOTS

This is my team's absolute favourite tofu dish, which is totally unexpected given that none of them had ever heard of 'tofu knots' before I first made it for them. To be fair, it is probably my favourite recipe in the book, too, and my most requested dish. Pretty, crisp and chewy, it is a show-stopper that delivers the most satisfying bite; nobody can believe that it is tofu. 'It tastes more chickeny than chicken,' is probably my favourite quote of all. (Thank you, Teresa!)

Tofu knots are often called 'bean curd knots' in Asian stores, and can usually be found in the aisle with other dried soup ingredients, as they are traditionally added to bulk up stews with their protein and texture, rather than fried until crispy as I do here.

Serves 2–3

For the tofu

100g/3½oz dried golden tofu knots, soaked in hot water for 1 hour, then drained

100g/3½oz/¾ cup cornflour (corn starch)

150ml/5fl oz/⅔ cup vegetable oil

toasted sesame seeds, to serve

spring onions (scallions), finely sliced, to serve

For the sauce

2 tbsp tomato ketchup

1 tbsp gochujang

3 tbsp clear honey

2 tbsp rice vinegar, malt vinegar or Worcestershire sauce

1 tbsp light soy sauce

1 tbsp toasted sesame oil

1. In a bowl, coat the softened tofu knots with the cornflour, until all the knobbly angles and curves are covered. Leave for 10 minutes to let the cornflour soak up the moisture around the tofu.

2. In a frying pan, heat the oil until bubbling-hot and add some of the tofu knots. Be sure not to crowd the pan; you may have to cook them in batches. After 2–3 minutes, flip them over. Some angles will be golden brown and crisping up. Keep turning them until each knot is crispy and golden. Drain on kitchen paper (paper towels). If you are not finishing the dish straight away, pop them into a medium oven to keep them warm and crispy.

3. Mix all the sauce ingredients together in a bowl, then put in a clean saucepan. Place over a medium heat until the sauce bubbles and starts to reduce.

4. Throw the crispy tofu knots into the sweet, sticky sauce and mix to coat, then serve immediately, scattered with toasted sesame seeds and spring onions.

TOFU & MUSHROOM DAN DAN NOODLES

Dan dan noodles are so satisfying. Thick, chewy noodles with a rich, crumbly topping and an invigorating spice that leaves your mouth a little bit tingly. The traditional Sichuanese recipe is fatty and juicy with pork mince, which is hard to replicate with tofu. However, dried tofu, with its chewy, bouncy texture works well. Flavours do not just politely coat the edges of the tofu, they are absorbed promptly, plumply and proudly. This dish takes some prep, but you can make a big batch of the tofu topping, as it keeps for up to a week in the refrigerator. If you cannot get hold of dried tofu, use chopped fried tofu or crumbled fresh tofu instead. The key to super-satisfying dan dan noodles is thick-cut noodles; seek out thick fresh wheat noodles at Asian stores, or, if you are using dried, go for thick, pure wheat noodles without any egg. The dressing can be kept in a sealed jar in the refrigerator for up to two weeks.

Serves 4

For the noodles

2 tbsp vegetable oil, plus 2 tsp

2 tsp whole Sichuan peppercorns,

8 dried shiitake mushrooms, soaked for 1–2 hours until fully hydrated, drained, then diced into 1cm/½ inch cubes

4 spring onions (scallions), finely sliced, plus extra to serve

200g/7oz dried tofu sticks, soaked in water for at least 4 hours, then drained and finely chopped

4 tbsp Sichuan preserved pickled vegetables, finely chopped

4 tsp rice wine

2 tbsp hoisin sauce, or sweet bean sauce

2 tsp dark soy sauce

660g/1lb 7oz fresh thick wheat noodles, or 400g/14oz thick dried wheat noodles (try to avoid egg noodles)

2 tbsp toasted sesame oil

2 garlic cloves, finely chopped

4 heads of pak choi (bok choy), quartered lengthways

handful of coriander (cilantro), chopped, to serve

chopped peanuts, to serve

For the dressing

2½ tbsp sesame paste or tahini

3 tbsp light soy sauce

2 tsp caster sugar (superfine sugar)

¼ tsp Chinese five spice

2 tsp Chinkiang vinegar

½ tsp ground Sichuan peppercorns

2 tbsp chilli oil with sediment

1. Heat the 2 tbsp of vegetable oil in a small saucepan over a low heat, add the peppercorns and toast for 6 minutes. Turn off the heat and leave to cool slightly, before removing the peppercorns, leaving the oil behind.

2. Warm the oil again, then add the shiitake mushrooms, spring onions and chopped tofu and stir around in the spicy oil.

3. Grind the peppercorns to a fine powder, then return them to the pan to allow the flavour of the spice to mingle into the tofu. Add the preserved pickled vegetables and cook for a further 2 minutes. Add the rice wine, hoisin sauce and dark soy sauce, stir-fry for a further 2 minutes, then turn off the heat.

4. Cook the noodles according to the packet instructions, rinse immediately, as the starchiness of the noodles will cause them to stick together, then dress straight away with the sesame oil to prevent them from sticking. Set aside.

5. In a small bowl, mix together all the dressing ingredients.

6. In a frying pan, heat the 2 tsp of vegetable oil and fry the garlic until lightly golden, then add the pak choi to cook through, stirring for 2 minutes over the heat, then switch the heat off and cover with a lid to steam through for 3–4 minutes.

7. To serve, lightly toss the noodles and pak choi with half the dressing and divide between 4 bowls. Leave the remainder of the dressing in a bowl on the side for guests to help themselves to more spicy sauce as they desire.

8. Top each bowl with a ladle of the tofu mushroom mixture and serve with chopped coriander, peanuts and spring onions on the side, so people can choose their own toppings.

MISO SOUP WITH ABURAAGE AND DEEP-FRIED AUBERGINE

This is a super-quick recipe for a richer miso soup. The silky pieces of unctuous aubergine (eggplant) and the satisfyingly chewy fried tofu add new textures to a classic miso soup.

Serves 4

200ml/7fl oz/generous ¾ cup vegetable oil

150g/5½oz aubergine (eggplant), cut into 1cm/½ inch cubes

750ml/1¼ pints/3 generous cups dashi (powdered, or see pages 27–8 for home-made), or vegetable stock

60g/2¼oz/4 tbsp white miso paste

100g/3½oz *aburaage* tofu

2 tsp finely chopped spring onions (scallions)

1. Fill a deep saucepan with the oil so that it is at least 2.5cm/1 inch deep, depending on the size of the pan (it should reach no more than one-third of the way up the sides). Heat until small bubbles start to appear. As always when deep-frying, be very careful and do not leave the kitchen or take a telephone call.

2. Fry the aubergine cubes in 2 batches, until golden on all sides and cooked through. This should take 2 or 3 minutes. Drain on kitchen paper (paper towels) to remove excess oil.

3. Meanwhile in another saucepan, heat up the dashi. When it is hot – but not boiling – remove a few tablespoons of it into a small bowl and mix with the miso. Return this mixture to the dashi pan. Simmer for 2 minutes, taking care not to boil it, as this can have a detrimental effect on the nutrients in the miso.

4. Slice the *aburaage* tofu into fine ribbons and add to the miso soup pan for 1 minute, before adding the aubergines. Serve immediately, scattered with the spring onions.

INARI SUSHI

Quite possibly the easiest sushi you can make at home. Inari sushi are pockets of seasoned deep-fried tofu stuffed with Japanese rice. The *aburaage* is made by simmering tofu pockets in a sweet and savoury broth that pairs beautifully with the rice stuffing. The two ingredients make a magic combo: sweet, nutty, savoury and chewy. The golden pouches are great for enjoying at home, on picnics or in lunchboxes, as they transport well, too. Tofu pockets can be bought in the chilled section at most Asian stores.

Makes 12

For the rice and tofu

485g/1lb 1oz/3 cups Japanese rice/ sushi rice

1 tbsp toasted sesame seeds, plus extra to serve

1. Cook the sushi rice according to the packet instructions (package directions) and leave to cool.

2. Combine the rice seasoning ingredients in a bowl, pour over the cooling rice and mix well. Add the toasted sesame seeds to the rice and allow it to cool to room temperature, fanning it to speed up the process.

12 store-bought *aburaage*

light soy sauce, to serve

pickled sushi ginger, to serve

For the rice seasoning

80ml/2¾fl oz/generous ¼ cup rice vinegar

3 tbsp caster sugar (superfine sugar)

1 tsp fine sea salt

3. Prepare a bowl of cold water and keep it to hand. Carefully open up the tofu pockets; they are quite fragile so do this slowly. Make a small ball of rice in your hands that will fit into a pocket. If your hands get sticky, wet them with water.

4. Stuff the rice into the tofu pocket until it is completely filled, then turn it upside down to stand up on a plate. Repeat for the rest of the inari, then sprinkle with sesame seeds before serving with a small dip of soy sauce and slivers of pickled ginger.

TOFU PUFF ATSUAGE WITH MISO CHIVE BUTTER

This dish was created by accident when I had leftover miso butter to use up and it became an instant hit! Tofu puffs are usually served in noodle soups and added to stews and hotpots, but are not often stir-fried. Here, the miso butter provides these savoury profiterole-like balls with chewy, crispy, caramelized edges and a soft centre. The sweet beany flavour of the tofu is intensified by the miso to give a tangy but sweet, funky flavour akin to cheese and onion crisps! Easily found in Asian stores, this is a quick and easy way to try tofu puffs: brilliant as a noodle topping, or simply with steamed rice.

Serves 4

40g 1½oz/2 generous tbsp white miso paste

50g/1¾oz/½ stick unsalted butter, softened, at room temperature

2 tbsp finely chopped chives, plus extra to serve

1 tbsp sunflower oil

200g/7oz packet (package) deep-fried tofu puffs (*atsuage*)

1. In a mixing bowl, blend together the miso and butter until completely smooth, then mix in the chives.

2. Heat the oil in a frying pan (skillet) and add the tofu, stirring every few minutes until all the sides are starting to turn darker in colour and the puffs begin to shrink.

3. Now add the miso butter to the pan, mixing it around the tofu with a spatula to ensure all the sides are coated.

4. Reduce the heat under the pan, as miso can burn easily, and move the tofu frequently, until all the butter has been absorbed. Serve immediately, sprinkled with another snip of chives.

NEW YEAR'S DAY TOFU

Originally created by Chinese Buddhist monks, this dish makes use of a number of fresh and dried vegan ingredients, and (despite the name) is enjoyed throughout the year.

Also known as Buddha's Delight, I much prefer the name New Year's Day tofu, as it conveys the important symbolism of this dish as you begin a new year. It is traditional in Chinese culture and other Asian societies to refrain from eating meat on New Year's Day as a sign of respect and a way of garnering good karma for the year ahead. Symbolically, the ingredients you choose for this dish represent different meanings, due to the way they look, or how their name is pronounced in the Chinese language. For example, bamboo shoots represent wealth and new beginnings, noodles stand for longevity, shiitake mushrooms symbolize opportunity, dried tofu refers to blessings to the house, and fried tofu represents gold bricks, no less! So don't hold back if you're getting ready to begin a new chapter; here's your chance to pave the way ahead.

If you don't have dried tofu to hand, fried tofu can make a simple replacement. There is some prep time involved in making this recipe, which simply involves soaking dried ingredients, but then the dish comes together quickly.

Serves 4

2 tbsp vegetable oil

3 garlic cloves, finely sliced

4 slices of peeled fresh ginger

8 dried shiitake mushrooms, soaked in hot water for 1–2 hours until fully hydrated, drained then sliced

100g/3½oz chinese leaf or cabbage, finely sliced

4 dried tofu sticks, soaked in hot water for 30 minutes, then drained and cut into 3–4cm/1¼–1½ inch pieces

30g/1oz/½ cup dried black fungus (wood ear mushrooms), soaked in water for 10–15 minutes, then drained and roughly sliced

100g/3½oz/generous ½ cup bamboo shoots

4 tbsp vegetarian mushroom sauce, or oyster sauce

2 tbsp Shaoxing rice wine

2 tsp light soy sauce

1 tsp toasted sesame oil

100g/3½oz bean thread noodles, soaked in boiling water

sea salt flakes and freshly ground white pepper

1. In a wok or large frying pan (skillet), heat up the oil and sauté the garlic and ginger for 2–3 minutes, then add the shiitake mushrooms and stir-fry for a further 3 minutes.

2. Add the Chinese cabbage and tofu sticks. The pan will feel overloaded but, once the cabbage cooks down, it will become manageable.

3. Add the black fungus and bamboo shoots to the pan.

4. In a small mixing bowl, stir together the mushroom or oyster sauce, rice wine, soy sauce and sesame oil and pour into the pan. The cabbage should have released moisture into the pan, but if the whole dish is a bit dry, add 2 tbsp water, then cover and steam for 5 minutes.

5. If you are adding bean thread noodles, this is the time, as you do not want them to be overcooked. Season with little salt and white pepper and serve.

TWISTS

Try adding other vegetables such as baby corn, straw mushrooms, mangetout (snow peas) or carrots.

SWEET TOFU

Tofu in desserts? Bear with me…

Silken tofu has the remarkable ability to transform into creamy textures similar to those of whipped ricotta, or wobbly pannacotta, so it is actually very adaptable for puddings once you know how. It brings a cloud-like lightness to traditionally heavier desserts, and provides a creamy canvas for sweet, stronger flavours to dance on.

In China, dried tofu is the star of many sweet soups (you'll find my favourite on page 136), while in Japan, the French influence in patisserie has created many fusion desserts that embrace classical Western techniques but with traditional Eastern ingredients such as creamy silken tofu, matcha and red beans.

My collection of tofu-based desserts here vary from classic Cantonese sweet staples to more inventive recipes that embrace tofu as a cream or milk alternative, for a lighter after-dinner experience.

CHOCOLATE RASPBERRY TOFU ICE CREAM

Dairy-free ice creams can be a bit hit and miss: sometimes they just aren't rich and creamy enough. Silken tofu to the rescue! It has the creamy consistency of whole milk but provides a neutral base upon which to build other flavours. Super-rich and creamy, this is an incredibly easy dessert that really does have the consistency of classic ice cream. The raspberries cut through its dense richness to achieve a happy balance. Make sure the chocolate you use is soya lecithin-free, or the ice cream may split.

Serves 8

310g/11oz/generous/1½ cups coconut oil

240g/8½oz/2 cups soya lecithin-free 70% dark chocolate, chopped (Willie's Cacao or Ritter Sport are good brands), plus extra to serve

780g/1lb 11oz silken tofu, beaten to a smooth cream

250g/9oz/1¼ cups caster sugar (superfine sugar)

6 tbsp cocoa powder (unsweetened cocoa)

1 tsp sea salt flakes

2 vanilla pods (vanilla beans), split lengthways

100g/3½oz/¾ cup raspberries, plus extra to serve

1. Start with 2 saucepans. In the first pan, melt the coconut oil, then allow it to cool slightly. Place another small saucepan, half-filled with boiling water, over a medium-low heat, then place a heatproof bowl on top, making sure the base doesn't touch the water. Put the chocolate in the bowl and stir every so often so it melts evenly.

2. Once the chocolate has melted, remove it from the heat and let it cool for 15 minutes.

3. Put the cooled melted chocolate into a large mixing bowl and add the beaten tofu, sugar, cocoa powder and salt. Mix together, then scrape the seeds from the vanilla pods into the mix.

4. Tip the ice cream mixture into a blender to purée until smooth (about 15–20 seconds).

5. Set the food processor speed to low and slowly stream in the coconut oil, as if you were making mayonnaise, just until the mix is thick and creamy, then stop. Beware: if you overblend, it starts to curdle and you will have to start again!

6. Immediately spoon into an ice cream machine and churn according to the manufacturer's instructions. Do not refrigerate first, or the oil will harden and the texture will be grainy. Note that this does take longer to set than a dairy ice cream. Stir in the raspberries.

7. Transfer the ice cream to an airtight container and press some clingfilm (plastic wrap) directly onto the surface. Freeze until firm, or for at least 4 hours.

8. Bring the ice cream out of the freezer for at least 15 minutes before serving, for the perfect soft scoop.

9. Serve it in a cone or bowl, with freshly grated chocolate and raspberries.

TWISTS

Try adding crunchy nuts and other fruits that work well with dark chocolate, such as blackberries, apricots, cherries, figs or cranberries.

BAKED MATCHA TOFU CHEESECAKE

A fun tofu take on a much-loved classic. The matcha tiger stripes bring a little drama, as well as bitterness against the familiar creamy body, while the tofu provides a smoothness that just melts in the mouth. One to impress your guests!

Serves 8

For the base

75g/2¾oz/scant ¾ stick unsalted butter, plus extra for the tin

150g/5½oz digestive biscuits (graham crackers)

For the filling

500g/1lb 2oz/2¼ cups cream cheese

2 large eggs, lightly beaten

175g/6oz/generous ¾ cup caster sugar (superfine sugar)

1 vanilla pod (vanilla bean), split lengthways, seeds scraped out

2 tsp lemon juice

350g/12oz firm tofu, drained for 20 minutes and patted dry

5 tsp matcha green tea powder

1. Preheat the oven to 180°C fan/ 200°C/400°F/gas mark 6. Butter the base of a 23cm/9 inch springform cake tin and line it with baking paper (parchment paper).

2. Place the biscuits in a sealed bag and crush with a rolling pin to fine crumbs, or simply use a food processor.

3. Melt the butter in a small saucepan and add the biscuit crumbs, stirring to combine. Press into the base of the prepared tin in an even layer, flattening it with your fingers until it is smooth.

4. Bake in the oven for 10 minutes until golden, then leave to cool.

5. In a large bowl, whip the cream cheese until smooth and creamy, then beat in the eggs. Add the sugar, vanilla seeds and lemon juice and mix well.

6. Blitz the tofu in a food processor to a hummus-like consistency, then add it to the cream cheese mix.

7. Spoon about 250g/9oz/1 cup of the mix into another bowl and sift in the matcha powder to avoid lumps. Mix thoroughly until totally smooth.

8. Pour half the pale tofu mix into the cake tin on the biscuit base to create an even layer, then add blobs of half the matcha mix in a square formation on top. Repeat with the remaining plain tofu mix and then with the remaining matcha mix.

9. To create the marbled pattern, use a knife to run through the top of the green blobs in straight lines.

10. Bake for 10 minutes, then reduce the oven temperature to 160°C fan/ 180°C/350°F/gas mark 4 and bake for a further 45 minutes.

11. Once the cooking is complete, turn the oven off, open the door of the oven and leave the cheesecake inside for 1 hour before serving. Keep it in the refrigerator and enjoy within 3–4 days.

TOFU FA PUDDING

As a kid, my father used to take me to a bakery in Chinatown that served hot baked buns and tofu fa pudding upstairs, and ran a busy Chinese medical clinic downstairs. Whenever there was some ailment in the family, I was asked to sit quietly in the bakery while the patient was seen to. I would happily nurse my bowl of tofu fa with delight, secretly bidding them to take their time.

The bakery has sadly since closed down, but I think of it often: piercing the creamy hot tofu pudding with a spoon that was a little too big for my hands, drizzling it liberally with sticky ginger syrup and admiring the entrepreneurial spirit of this bakery-medical combo; serving remedies for both tummies and souls.

Serves 6–8

For the pudding

125g/4½oz/generous ½ cup dried soya beans, soaked overnight, then drained

2 litres/3½ pints/2.1 quarts water, plus 120ml/4fl oz/½ cup

5g/⅛oz agar agar powder

finely crushed peanuts, to serve (optional)

For the sweet ginger syrup

120ml/4fl oz/½ cup water

100g/3½oz/generous ½ cup brown sugar

2.5cm/1 inch fresh ginger, peeled and chopped

1. Rinse the soya beans, then, in a food processor, blend them and the 2 litres/3½ pints/2.1 quarts of water until all visible lumps have gone and the mixture is smooth.

2. Transfer to a large saucepan and bring to the boil, then reduce the heat to a simmer and cook for 45 minutes, until the soya milk thickens.

3. Pour the milk through a muslin cloth (cheesecloth) to strain out any residue and squeeze all the liquid into a large bowl. Pour it all back into the (cleaned) large saucepan and return to the boil, then switch off the heat.

4. In another large saucepan, bring the 120ml/4fl oz/½ cup of water to a rolling boil, then add the agar agar and stir until dissolved, ensuring the agar agar is boiled for 1–2 minutes to activate it. Add the soya milk to the pan and continue boiling for another 2–3 minutes.

5. Strain the mixture for a final time through a muslin cloth into a large bowl. Allow to cool, then cover and place in the refrigerator for at least 2 hours to set.

6. To make the sweet ginger syrup, bring the water to the boil, add the sugar and stir until dissolved. Add the ginger, then remove from the heat and allow to infuse for 1 hour. Strain out the ginger.

7. Once the tofu pudding is set, use a large ladle to scoop into each bowl, then add a spoon of ginger syrup. Finely crushed peanuts are also a popular addition, for extra texture, if you like.

TWISTS

If you would like to make Tofu Fa from soya milk rather than soya beans, then replace the soya beans and water with 2.5 litres/4½ pints/2.2 quarts of shop-bought soya milk. Use one with a higher soya bean concentration for a richer flavour. You will need to increase the amount of agar to 7g/¼oz as well.

SWEET TOFU SOUP

This dessert is seriously nostalgic for me. A sweet warming soup made from silky sheets of dried tofu, with a boiled egg or gingko nuts bobbing up and down, waving to be saved. It is a popular Cantonese snack and was a real treat for me as a child, when segments of orange were usually as much as I could expect after dinner! The dried tofu pieces melt tenderly into the sweet soup to create a creamy broth that still feels nourishing. Made in less than 10 minutes, I can see why my busy grandma would choose this as her go-to quick dessert for special occasions, made with storecupboard ingredients. In my recipe, I have used quail's eggs for a daintier dish, and I also love a little grating of nutmeg to enhance the eggy flavours.

It is important to buy dried tofu *sheets* for this recipe, not the dried tofu sticks, which are thicker in consistency. This is key to the creamy texture, as the sheets are extra thin, for melting down easily.

You can buy rock sugar in Asian stores, or online.

Serves 4–6

1.2 litres/2 pints/1 quart water
125g/4½oz/generous ½ cup rock
   sugar, or soft light brown sugar
1 teaspoon minced fresh ginger
150g/5½oz dried tofu skins
8–12 cooked quail's eggs
freshly grated nutmeg (optional)

1. Heat the water in a large saucepan until it is boiling, then add the sugar and ginger. Stir until the sugar has fully dissolved.

2. Break up the tofu skins with your hands and cook for 3–5 minutes until they are halfway melted into the soup. If you like a creamier soup, cook for an additional 3 minutes for the tofu skins to break down further.

3. For the last minute or so, warm up the quail's eggs in the soup.

4. Serve in small warmed bowls, adding a small grating of nutmeg if you wish.

TOFU DOUGHNUTS WITH MISO CARAMEL

I'm not going to lie, these are very naughty. Inspired by my love for ricotta doughnuts – light and fluffy and a tiny bit tart – these tofu doughnuts have a sweet and tangy flavour that really hits the spot.

The miso caramel is optional… but if you're going to the effort of making doughnuts, why hold back?

Serves 6–8

For the doughnuts

vegetable oil, for deep-frying and oiling

275g/9¼oz firm tofu, drained for 20 minutes, pressed (see pages 14–15), then mashed

1 tbsp lemon juice

finely grated zest of 1 lemon

2 tbsp nutritional yeast flakes

1 tsp sea salt flakes

3 eggs, lightly beaten

100g/3½oz/½ cup caster sugar (superfine sugar)

275g/9¼oz/generous 2 cups plain flour (all-purpose flour)

2 tsp baking powder

golden caster sugar (superfine sugar), for dusting

For the miso caramel (optional)

125ml/4fl oz/½ cup water

300g/10½oz/1½ cups granulated sugar

125g/4½oz/½ cup double cream (heavy cream)

1½ tbsp white miso paste

1. Prepare a very large saucepan (or deep-fat fryer) in which you will be deep-frying. Fill it with oil to come no more than one-third of the way up the sides and set it on to heat. It needs to reach 170°C/340°F. As always when deep-frying, be very careful and do not leave the kitchen or take a telephone call.

2. Layer a tray with kitchen paper (paper towels) for receiving your piping-hot doughnuts.

3. In a bowl, mix together the mashed tofu, lemon juice and zest, nutritional yeast, salt, beaten eggs and sugar.

4. Sift in the flour and baking powder, then fold together, taking care not to overwork the dough.

5. Oil an ice-cream scoop and make 25g/1oz balls of the dough. Drop 3 balls of batter into the hot oil and fry for 4–5 minutes, until golden brown. Turn occasionally to ensure the doughnuts are golden all over.

6. Remove from the oil with a slotted spoon and place on the paper-lined tray to blot off excess oil, then dust with golden caster sugar. Repeat to cook and coat all the doughnuts.

7. If you are making the miso caramel, heat the water and sugar in a heavy-based pan. Don't be tempted to stir it, or you might crystallize the caramel. Once the caramel is a dark golden brown, turn off the heat and leave to cool for a few minutes before slowly adding the cream and miso paste (be careful, as it may spit at you).

8. Serve the doughnuts with the caramel, dipping them into it, or drizzling it over, as you prefer.

TWISTS

The caramel can be stored in a refrigerator for up to a week. It is great on cakes and also drizzled on ice cream.

SILKEN TOFU CHOCOLATE MOUSSE WITH CHILLI

This is the dessert to make when you have forgotten about making a dessert. Having a pack of silken tofu in the cupboard on standby means you can quickly whip up this super-simple pudding that is deeply chocolatey and glossy, and also dairy-free.

If you want to make this a little bit extra, add something crunchy on top when you serve it, such as praline, or even a crumbled chocolate-covered honeycomb bar.

Makes 6

700g/1lb 9oz silken tofu

200g/7oz/1¼ cups 70% cocoa dark chocolate, broken or chopped

160g/5¾oz/¾ cup maple syrup

finely grated zest of 1 lime

seeds from 1 vanilla pod (vanilla bean), or 1 tsp vanilla extract

large pinch of chilli flakes

large pinch of sea salt, plus extra to serve

finely grated orange zest, to serve (optional)

1. First, drain the tofu in a sieve while you prepare the rest of the ingredients.

2. Place a small saucepan, half-filled with boiling water, over a medium-low heat, then place a heatproof bowl on top, making sure the base doesn't touch the water. Put the chocolate in the bowl and stir every so often so it melts evenly. Leave to cool for about 15 minutes.

3. Using a food processor, blitz the tofu with the remaining ingredients, except the chocolate, for 1–2 minutes until smooth.

4. Add the melted chocolate and pulse-blend until silky and combined.

5. Divide the mixture between 6 little bowls (200ml/7fl oz/¾ cup each) and leave to set in the refrigerator for at least 2 hours.

6. Serve with some grated orange zest and another pinch of sea salt.

FROZEN TOFU
PEANUT BUTTER PIE

A sweet tart inspired by a dessert I once tried in a cafe in Ipoh, Malaysia. The achingly sweet peanut butter is tempered by the coconut cream and silken tofu. Serve cold with a cup of coffee, or, if you can find it, Malaysian black *kopi*.

Serves 8

For the base

75g/2¾oz/about 5 tbsp unsalted butter, plus more for the dish

200g/7oz Hobnobs or similar crumbly oat biscuits (cookies)

For the filling

350g/12oz silken tofu, drained and patted dry

85g/3oz/scant ½ cup maple syrup

125g/4½oz/generous ½ cup smooth peanut butter

1–2 tsp fine sea salt, depending on the salt level of the peanut butter

100ml/3½fl oz/scant ½ cup coconut cream

80ml/2½fl oz/5 tbsp soya milk, or regular milk

100g/3½oz/generous ½ cup chocolate chips

roasted salted peanuts, crushed, for the topping

1. Preheat the oven to 190°C fan/ 210°C/410°F/gas mark 6–7.

2. Butter a pie dish around 20cm/ 8 inches in diameter.

3. Place the biscuits in a sealed bag and crush with a rolling pin to fine crumbs, or simply use a food processor.

4. Melt the butter in a small saucepan and add the biscuit crumbs, stirring to combine. Press into the base of the prepared tin in an even layer, flattening it with your fingers until it is smooth.

5. Bake in the oven for 10 minutes until golden, then leave to cool.

6. Put the tofu, maple syrup and peanut butter in a blender and process on a slow speed for 2 minutes until thick and creamy. Add salt to taste.

7. Take the coconut cream and whip it in a bowl until soft, then fold it into the tofu mix.

8. Pour the filling over the biscuit base and freeze for 1 hour, while you prepare the topping.

9. Heat the milk at a low simmer for 4 minutes, then turn off the heat and pour it over the chocolate chips in a heatproof bowl. Wait for 3 minutes, then stir it together into a ganache.

10. Spoon over the pie in an even layer, working quickly to avoid the ganache cooling down and clumping.

11. Top evenly with crushed roasted salted peanuts, then set in the freezer for 20–30 minutes before serving. It will keep in the refrigerator for up to 4 days.

INDEX